To every teacher who has ever forgotten to listen during a meeting, to every student who has ever felt confused during a lecture and to little Charlie, who despite valiant attempts to pay attention, eventually fell asleep during 'carpet time'.

Contents

Introduction

What is Talk-Less Teaching?

When well-known comedians take to the stage, they face an audience full of avid listeners. They look down at a sea of eager faces, each belonging to a devoted fan who has paid for the privilege of drinking in their every word. Sometimes a lesson can feel like that for the teacher and the learners. Sometimes – but not always.

Imagine for a moment that the topic the stand-up intends to talk about isn't especially amusing. Imagine that it isn't familiar or even apparently relevant to the audience's frames of reference. Imagine that rather than having paid for the privilege of listening, the audience are there by obligation. Perhaps they are small children with ants in their pants or teenagers who have more 'important' things to be thinking about. Imagine, just imagine, that the comedian isn't a born entertainer whose mere facial expressions are enough to induce rapture and delight. Would the audience still listen attentively, absorb, understand and remember everything the stand-up said?

This imagined scenario is far closer to the reality of a classroom. It's a brave teacher, indeed, who would assume that their 'audience' is capable of listening attentively to and taking in every part of a 30-minute speech. This won't stop the odd teaching colleague from telling you, 'There's nothing wrong with talking to a class all lesson if that's the only way to get the information across to them!' The problems with this theory are tenfold:

1   It is never the *only* way to get the information across, as the strategies in this book will demonstrate.

2   Talking can be the quickest way to impart information (so it can feel like the most efficient and satisfying way) but it is often not the most effective way to secure understanding and embed it in the long term.

3   The 'turn-up-and-teach' method is sometimes misused as an alternative to thoughtful planning – which means differentiation (among other aspects of good teaching) goes out the window.

4   It's impossible to get feedback from your learners about what they are understanding while you are the one doing the talking. So, if you talk for a long period of time, you run the risk of subsequently discovering that not only have some learners not understood you, but others haven't been actively listening at all.

5   If you're observing someone else's lesson for personal development or performance management purposes, you'll know that, as long as the teacher is talking, you have no gauge to assess the impact of that teaching. You will remain completely ignorant of whether learners are actually listening, and therefore making progress by gaining new knowledge and eliminating misconceptions.

6   This theory is often offered by that colleague who has always liked the sound of their own voice, and doesn't realise that not everyone else around them feels the same.

7   This theory is sometimes offered by Mr or Mrs Charisma Incarnate. This is the colleague who probably could have been one of the celebrated comedians mentioned above, but having taken to the classroom, has only to open their mouth to have every single learner mesmerised. It's easy for this person to mistakenly believe that every colleague around them possesses the same rare gift.

8   Having to listen to someone speak for a long period of time can cause an audience to feel restless and rebellious.

9   The longer the teacher talks for, the less time learners have to think for themselves, and the less time there remains for learners to ask questions they need answers to or discuss concepts so that they can understand them better.

10 Adhering to this theory can result in a sore throat.

Point number 7 is a particularly important one: outstanding teachers come in all sorts of shapes and sizes. There is no one way to teach a lesson, no single style that beats all the other styles hands down. As long as our learners are making fabulous progress, then we should stick with what we're doing (unless it's mind control or lobotomy).

Reduced teacher-talk is not desirable in essence. It is desirable to reduce teacher-talk when it is getting in the way of learners making the best progress that they can and when it is getting in the way of making learning meaningful, purposeful and, dare we say, even enjoyable at times. So, teacher-talk should only be viewed negatively if it is of poor quality or if it is impeding pupil progress. If you're confident that you're one of those gifted orators who can get every single learner in your class making progress through talking to them for long periods of time, or if you have a class made up entirely of learners with exceptional auditory processing skills who are indisputably benefitting from your lectures and have little need to practise the skills or use the knowledge that you are telling them about, then go ahead and talk till the cows come home. For the rest of us, we need to have a sizeable bank of alternative strategies up our sleeve to help learners to stay motivated, understand difficult concepts and make visible progress. This is what you will find in this book.

Of course, you may be reading this book because you want to help colleagues who, for one or more of the reasons above, are unwittingly impeding pupil progress through an excess of teacher-talk or inadvertently turning people off from learning through requiring them to be passive recipients – not just occasionally but on a daily basis. There are plenty of ideas in the chapters that follow to support teachers of any year group, and of any subject, to engage and enthuse their classes so that learners take responsibility for their own learning, and so that progress is highly visible and measurable. In fact, the strategies in this book are specifically designed to stop learners from relying on an apathetic takeaway approach to school ('You do it all for me and I'll pick up the nice grade at the end, thank you very much'). Instead, the practical strategies we outline support a *MasterChef* approach to school, where every learner is encouraged to be responsible for their own progress, and to use and practise what they learn with increasing confidence and skill.

Because that, dear teacher friends, is what talk-less teaching is all about: a way of teaching that engages and involves every learner, offers a variety of experiences in the classroom and has a demonstrable impact on the quality of lessons and on pupil progress. Talk-less teaching can improve outcomes for learners from nursery to university. Talk-less teaching shows you how to foster active and independent learning without compromising exam results or knowledge acquisition. It is all about making sure we have realistic, practical ways to help learners understand difficult concepts and learn new skills without making the poor dears listen incessantly to the sound of our voices, and to raise attainment without resorting to mind-numbing and formulaic teaching-to-the-test.

But talk-less teaching is much more than that. From the thousands of teachers with whom we've worked, one response in particular has chimed out above all others: talk-less teaching makes teaching *irresistible*. It doesn't just put the delight back into the learners' experience, it makes teaching thoroughly enjoyable too.

So, to fully appreciate the wonder of strategies which do not require long periods of passive listening, let's start by putting ourselves into the shoes of the people we teach …

The best way to do this is to consider a typical staff meeting. Now, it should be fair to assume that the agenda in these meetings is pretty important (latest test results, changes to the curriculum, health and safety, etc.), but who among us has not, at one time or another, despite their best efforts to concentrate, experienced a scenario similar to the following:

Chairperson: If you look at page 4 of the document, you'll see that … blah, blah, blah.

Your brain: The refreshments at meetings have really gone downhill since Janet left. I miss those little pink wafer things we always used to get … I wonder if she used to get them from that little shop in …

Chairperson: John! Did you want to mention anything about that problem?

Your brain: Argh! I stopped listening! What is he referring to? Think! … No – just look pensive … And pray that someone else chips in!

Your mouth: Um. No, I don't think so.

Your brain: Oh. My. Goodness. Now I look like a complete imbecile. [Brain continues along this line of thought for another five minutes while the chairperson continues to talk.]

No one can deny that it's extremely easy for our minds to wander when all we're required to do is listen. Even if we know we genuinely *need* to listen. It's the same if we are given something repetitive and easy to do – our minds wander while we do it. However, get us to do something that requires us to be *active* and *mindful,* and our attention is suddenly captured.

Try This ...

Use a video camera to film a lesson. Focus the camera on the learners rather than on the teacher. Look out for elements of the learners' body language and facial expressions that indicate levels of engagement and attentiveness.

What do you notice about the levels of learner engagement when the teacher is addressing the class, compared to those when the learners are required to be actively doing something other than listening?

At which points of the lesson do you see the most yawns occurring?

While the learners are required to take in information aurally, are there any indications that some learners may not be listening or understanding?

You may have experienced the potential strain of 'sitting and listening' during staff development training. This is another common experience that we teachers share with students when we are occasionally required to be passive recipients of new learning; that is, we are required to listen to someone speak for a relatively long period of time. There are a number of reasons why we might not always get the best out of this passive listening experience and these can be directly compared to the experience of learners in our own lessons.

A learner's experience in a lesson		Your experience at a staff development event
The learner has already decided, before the lesson begins, that this topic is not relevant to them. They don't see where they would ever need this skill in later life or they may not have opted to do this subject and have written it off as a waste of time.		You are tempted to bring your huge pile of marking to the staff training event because you have a million-and-one things that you could be getting on with, including your corridor display, lesson planning, report writing, etc.

A learner's experience in a lesson		Your experience at a staff development event
The learner is adamant that, because of what they perceive to be their particular circumstances or personal difficulties, the teacher will never be able to make the work accessible to them. Therefore, any attempts at attentive listening will be futile.		You feel that there is something particularly special about the subject or year group that you teach and therefore you already anticipate that a generic INSET will never be relevant to your particular circumstance.
The learner believes that what their teacher has to say is just 'more of the same', and therefore they are inclined to switch off because they don't anticipate learning anything new or interesting.		You are an experienced teacher and are convinced that you have heard it all before because 'initiatives in schools always come round full circle every few years'.
The learner listens attentively but just doesn't 'get it'. Since the teacher is unaware of their misconceptions, the learner leaves the lesson in a state of confusion and despair.		You leave an INSET about 'The Quality of Teacher-Talk', feeling confused and outraged that you must now conduct all your lessons through mime!
The learner has every intention of taking in new information through the art of careful listening, but they are distracted by the behaviour of another learner.		You try valiantly to take in what the speaker is saying and take relevant notes, but you are constantly distracted by the colleague next to you who wants to tell you about their recent meeting with the deputy head.

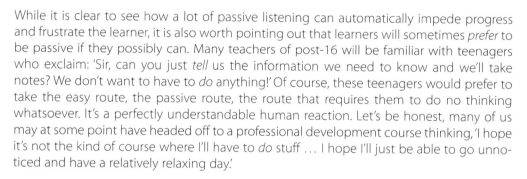

A learner's experience in a lesson		Your experience at a staff development event
The very able learner is naturally curious and their brain is generating umpteen questions as the teacher talks, but they have no opportunity to pursue these lines of enquiry further. Their hunger for clarification and elaboration is unfed, and they feel restless and thwarted by the situation.	→	You have 'jiggling leg syndrome' and are restless from the moment you sit down because you have a hundred questions you'd like to ask, and points you'd like to make, but the speaker is not allowing any opportunities for you to do this.

While it is clear to see how a lot of passive listening can automatically impede progress and frustrate the learner, it is also worth pointing out that learners will sometimes *prefer* to be passive if they possibly can. Many teachers of post-16 will be familiar with teenagers who exclaim: 'Sir, can you just *tell* us the information we need to know and we'll take notes? We don't want to have to *do* anything!' Of course, these teenagers would prefer to take the easy route, the passive route, the route that requires them to do no thinking whatsoever. It's a perfectly understandable human reaction. Let's be honest, many of us may at some point have headed off to a professional development course thinking, 'I hope it's not the kind of course where I'll have to *do* stuff … I hope I'll just be able to go unnoticed and have a relatively relaxing day.'

What we need to remember in this scenario is that while some of our learners might prefer to be passive in every lesson, it is important that we don't allow them to dictate to us how we teach. As the educational experts, *we* know that if they sit passively taking notes, do little thinking for themselves, ask no questions and make no attempts to develop their learning further or challenge themselves, then it is highly unlikely that they will achieve their potential – not just in the upcoming exam, but in life too! Similarly, a class full of 4- and 5-year-olds can frequently be beside themselves with excitement at the prospect of watching a film in their lesson, but this does not mean that they will learn more from sitting passively watching a TV screen than they will from role-playing, enquiring and actively investigating.

It's no secret that human beings learn and embed their learning most successfully by *doing* and being *actively involved* in their learning. We have only to take the example of learning to cook. If we had never cooked before and someone were to sit and tell us how to prepare a Sunday roast, it would be very difficult to replicate what we had just been

told, and even harder to remember it the next day. However, if we were allowed to *experiment*, *discover* for ourselves what worked and what didn't, *discuss* things as we went along, *collaborate*, *watch* and *do*, then we are likely to be able to produce increasingly tasty roast dinners for years to come. Learners can achieve their absolute best in this way – if we expect it of them, believe in them and persevere.

> **To put it bluntly, learning delivered primarily through teacher-talk is often the *easiest* option for both learners and teachers. It usually requires the least planning (assuming the teacher's subject knowledge is good) and it releases learners from an obligation to think, practise and explore.**

It's hardly surprising then that, with so much work to get through, the busy teacher can often find themselves over-relying on teacher-talk as the quickest way to impart learning. However, as your car's sat-nav sometimes fails to realise, the shortest route is not always the best route – especially when there are roadblocks and gaps in the road ahead.

Our anxiety to 'get through the syllabus' is usually the overriding reason why our automatic talk buttons get stuck in the 'on' position. It is a widely accepted notion that students' success can be measured by their performance in standardised tests and exams, and so, by extension, the competence of their teachers can be similarly assessed. When there is a whole lot of crucial content to cover, our default method for conveying information and skills to our learners is to talk … and talk … and talk. It's a natural human instinct: what do most of us do when we're anxious or under pressure? We talk – ten to the dozen. And, let's face it, we teachers are under huge amounts of pressure most of the time.

How many times have you heard inspirational and innovative colleagues lament the fact that they 'simply don't have time to use creative or engaging teaching strategies any more because there just isn't room in the syllabus to make the learning enjoyable'? There is a pervasive notion that vast amounts of test-related information must be transferred or 'uploaded' from teacher to learner, and that the best way to effect this transfer is through the power of talk. Any alternative method would amount to 'stopping' and wasting time in an already tight schedule.

So, the commonly experienced 'lecture laryngitis' that results from talking too much to our classes isn't necessarily a sign of an uninspiring teacher who doesn't care about making learning intriguing and exciting. In fact, it is far more likely, we believe, to be a symptom of that understandable fear that if we talk *less* in lessons, it will be impossible to get across all the vital information needed by learners to succeed.

Of course, most teachers acknowledge that didactic, lecture-style teaching fosters a culture of passivity in learners, where learners come to expect to have learning 'fed' to them – to be told the answers, rather than taught the skills to discover the answers themselves or even consider the possibility of alternative answers. However, despite active, independent learning being an unarguably worthy concept in itself, we can still feel that we're stuck in an impossible bind between, on the one hand, building independent learning skills, and on the other, cramming the content necessary to get the results on which we (and our learners) are ultimately judged. The upshot? We are still at risk of allowing lessons to be dominated by the sound of our own voices.

Most teachers have experienced that utter sense of exhaustion that can descend at the end of a busy day in the classroom – that moment when the last learner exits the room and we sink dejectedly into our chair, nursing a sore throat. It's a moment that should be filled with a warm feeling of satisfaction for a job well done, but often the overriding thought that creeps naggingly into our brain is: 'Hold on … did I just do almost *all* of the work back there? Did I just bust a gut for a whole hour only to get my pupils to do a tiny bit of work?' This realisation is then usually followed by a further insidious thought: 'What if it turns out that some of them only *looked* like they were listening? What if I take their books in and it turns out I just wasted all that time?'

> It will sometimes be necessary for learners to be passive recipients of their learning, but if they come to expect their schooling to take this form on a daily basis then they will become experts in the takeaway approach and never aspire to *MasterChef* status.

The sad fact is that most of us will, at certain points in our career, have uttered something similar to the following:

'No, Jemima, I will not draw the people for you just because you say you're "rubbish at drawing".'

'Daniel, why didn't you just ask for a pen instead of sitting there doing nothing?'

'Sophie, if you and Letitia really didn't understand, you could have asked for help, rather than chatting about boy bands.'

'Oscar, you've seen this word before. Don't wait for me to tell you it – try to sound it out.'

'Why did you all stop working just because I had to talk to Mr Hopps for two minutes?!'

'How about if I do the first bit for you? Will that help?'

'Henry, I have practically told you exactly what to write in my written comments! Why have you not made these changes in your final draft?'

'Stacey, please don't expect Mrs Teeay to do it all for you. She's here to help you, not to do your work for you!'

'Jonathan, I understand that you weren't sure about that question, but if you had just written *something* you might have picked up a couple of marks.'

'Penny, you can't be stuck already because you haven't tried yet. How can you know you can't do it if you haven't even tried?'

What we need is to feel confident in the *truth* that we can foster a classroom culture of independent thinking *and* improve progress and performance – yes, in tests too – by using teaching techniques which allow learning to go far deeper than it does when it is mostly administered aurally. What we need are techniques which protect against the potential for information to go 'in one ear and out the other' and which intrinsically motivate learners to learn. What we need is a vast bank of exciting, engaging, practical ways to allow learners to access and understand complex topics and skills without relentlessly bending their ears.

So, next time those learners look at you as if to say 'Talk to the blank stare, 'cos the brain ain't listening,' here's what you do: take a deep breath, remind yourself that there is another way and use the strategies in the following chapters to get the learners working harder than you, thinking harder than you and talking harder than you.

Chapter 1

The Chameleon Teacher

Tailoring Your Teaching to the Needs of Every Learner

If we're going to know for sure that learners are making genuine progress in our lessons, then we need to establish a starting point from which that progress can be measured. In other words, before we begin, we need to have an accurate understanding of learners' prior knowledge in relation to the topic we are teaching. Sometimes this important element of successful teaching and learning can be overlooked and we can instead resort to simply making an assumption about the starting point of our class.

A great teacher doesn't swan into the classroom with a second-by-second lesson plan and stick to it religiously, regardless of whether the learners are responding well or not. A great teacher doesn't drop in a quick 'progress check' or mini-plenary just for the sake of it and ignore what the exercise reveals about the understanding or skill of their learners. No, a great teacher craves any evidence they can get to assess the impact that their teaching is having, and they use this to inform how they teach their learners subsequently.

A great teacher assesses the impact of their teaching as they go along and adapts their teaching according to the information they glean. A great teacher is a readily flexible, ultra-adaptable 'chameleon teacher'.

A key element of talk-less teaching is about getting to know our learners better – what makes them tick, what helps them to understand and what their natural 'roadblocks' are. The less time we spend talking, the more time we have to ascertain this useful information. What pairings would work best for this particular activity? What specific examples are really capturing their interest? Who is already streets ahead with this topic? What part of this task are they struggling with most?

Talking less to our classes doesn't mean that we will be withholding vital information or being obtuse and unapproachable. On the contrary, to forge the best working relationships with our classes, we need to spend more time listening and creating opportunities for two-way communication. Of course, we know how all-important feedback is in the classroom, but we must remember that feedback in the classroom doesn't simply mean the constructive, diagnostic advice that the teacher gives the learners. There is, arguably, an even more important type of feedback that occurs in the classroom: the feedback that we teachers get from the learners about what they are taking in, remembering and understanding.

It is this feedback *from* the learners that should act as one of the greatest influences on our planning and delivery. This goes far beyond accessibility. We are not just talking about pitching the challenge at the correct level, but also about eliciting feedback about all the other vital elements of learning.

- Are there any adverse learning behaviours that could be rectified through an alternative approach to the lesson?

- Are there any learners who are not actively involved? How can they be drawn into the learning?

- Have I 'hooked' the class? How can I better engage their interest in the topic?

- Does the class have access to the right support materials? Are they asking questions that could be answered with an additional resource rather than depending on the teacher?

- Are there any pockets of learners that require additional support?

- Is the task I have planned for the learners coming together as I had hoped? Would it be beneficial to adjust the length or breadth?

Try This …

In the staffroom, sit and talk to someone you don't know very well. Spend about five minutes telling them about your experiences of teaching, your challenges and achievements. Don't leave any gaps in your monologue. After five minutes of explaining this to them, consider the following:

- How much have you found out about your colleague's struggles or triumphs in the classroom?

- What have you learnt about what you could do to help your colleague?

- How do you know whether your colleague understands what you have explained?

OK, so we're being a bit facetious here – but you get the general message. If you have just engaged in that cringe-worthy conversation with a colleague, you will have found that you got some frustration out of your system and gave yourself an opportunity to toot your own horn, but you will have received no answers to the probing questions above. Your own monopoly of the talking time will have prevented you from getting any feedback (and from making any new friends in the staffroom!).

All of this brings us to a potentially uncomfortable revelation: plenaries do not belong exclusively at the end of a lesson. We can't risk waiting until the last 10 minutes to check on understanding, only to discover that half the class just haven't 'got it'. This may be an uncomfortable revelation because many of you will remember that for years, the good old National Strategy had us all exploding into a flurry of Q&As, presentations, evaluations and, no doubt in some cases, *ritual chanting* at exactly 10 minutes before the bell. Deeply ingrained though this practice might be, it's time to step away from formulaic, prescriptive lesson structures and claim back the greatest skill we teachers have: *great professional judgement*. It is our professional judgement that will allow us to see when progress and understanding need to be checked, and consequently when and where we need to intervene to support and stretch our learners.

For example, our great professional judgement should tell us never, ever to interrupt learners who are busy making progress, simply to 'prove' the progress they are making!

Being a Chameleon Teacher

You may well have heard the famous assertion that to progress into being a 'good' teacher you need to *tighten* up, but to move from 'good' to 'outstanding' teaching you need to *loosen* up. What this aphorism highlights is just how important it is that, once we have ascertained information about our learners' prior knowledge, we use that knowledge to teach accordingly.

This can feel like a rather courageous mission at times. Of course, we will have a core plan for our lessons, but being a chameleon teacher can sometimes mean acknowledging that we will have to go into a scheme of work feeling a little 'blinder' than we would wish, and then think on our feet when it comes to the delicate, responsive selection of activity and focus for each learner.

Helping learners to make sustained progress requires frequent evaluation of their level of skill, knowledge or understanding, so that we can subsequently set just the right tasks to help them move onwards and upwards. In this chapter you'll find plenty of practical strategies to help you do just that.

Begin at the Beginning

By establishing the all-important starting point, any pupil progress made in your lesson will be far more visible to you and to the learners themselves. This is crucial, both for allowing you to assess the impact of your teaching on pupil progress, and for enabling learners to feel motivated by and proud of the headway they're making. Remember that, unless you're teaching a class full of identically programmed robots, this starting point will differ from learner to learner. Therefore, individuals' outcomes at the end of the lesson (or series of lessons) need to be measured against each individual's original starting point.

Of course, we'll usually find out very quickly if we've pitched the level of challenge inappropriately high (learners' blank stares and multiple mutterings of 'I don't get it' are a fairly good giveaway). At some point, most of us have had the experience of planning to illuminate a skill, such as writing a formal letter, only to discover five minutes in that some of the learners don't even know where they live, let alone how to spell their address. What is far harder to spot, however, is when a task has *underestimated* a learner's prior knowledge. In these situations, the learner may complete an activity with great aplomb, but what genuine, measurable progress will have been made in their skill, knowledge or understanding?

We can't measure progress unless we first establish a starting point from which to measure it. This is a fact that is easily forgotten or ignored because it's far simpler to assume a common starting point, and teach to the middle, than it is to provide a differentiated learning journey for every child. The indisputable reality, however, is that Naheed has a far better grasp of events in *Macbeth* than Jordan does (because Naheed's father once took her to see a theatre production of it), and Henry knows more about serving in tennis than Jasmine does (because there's a tennis court behind his house).

Kick Off

Once you have a clear idea of the position from which each of your learners will be kicking off, you are ideally positioned to see exactly how to help each learner make genuine progress. Your initial 'needs analysis' will enable you to ascertain where the gaps in understanding and knowledge are for various groups of learners in your class, so you can ensure that the learning activities you use will target those gaps with impressive precision. But how do we conduct this all-important needs analysis?

KWL is a well-known way to help learners to see and celebrate their learning journey over a lesson (or series of lessons). Standing for *Know*, *Wonder* (or Want to know) and *Learnt*, this acronym lends itself well to the establishing of a starting point from which progress can subsequently be measured at the end of a lesson or unit of work.

Asking learners to articulate what they know at the beginning of a topic is clearly a must. Asking them to review what they have learnt at the end is similarly crucial. Asking them what they are 'wondering' can sometimes feel a little dangerous, as we may be nervous that their curiosity and pondering will become irrelevant and throw the lesson off track. However, ascertaining and celebrating learners' 'wondering questions' can be a valuable activity and cause progress to occur in unexpected ways. It can also go a long way to giving learners the motivation they need to investigate and think about a topic more carefully.

Gathering learners' questions and queries is also, obviously, an effective way of establishing current levels of knowledge and understanding. Doing this at the beginning of a lesson, and then allowing learners to answer their original questions at the end, is a useful technique to make the learners' progress highly visible to themselves. Of course, this will only work if, having ascertained their needs at the beginning of the lesson, you use your chameleon teacher skills to ensure that the teaching and learning that ensues helps them to close those gaps!

There are many fun and effective ways to collect questions from your learners (there are lots more ideas for doing this in Chapter 5). In the meantime, here is a particularly useful one to help you tailor your teaching to the needs of your learners from the very outset of a lesson or scheme of work.

Strategy: The Wonderball

Those of you who have read *Pimp Your Lesson!*, and are already well-practised in the benefits of inflatable fun in the classroom, will enjoy this useful activity immensely.[1] Simply follow these easy instructions:

1   Share with learners the topic or 'core objective' that they are going to be working on in this lesson or unit of work.

2   Give each individual, pair or group a sticky note and ask them to write down one question they have about the topic or objective at this early stage in the lesson. In effect, what you are asking them to do here is to *personalise* the learning objective. In other words, you have told them what the overarching goal is and you are asking them to consider what *they, in particular,* will need to do, find out more about or get clarified in order to reach that goal themselves. This emphasises two things for the learners: first, the fact that while the core lesson objective may be the same for everyone, personal targets mean each learner will need to make a slightly different 'journey' to get there; and second, each learner needs to take responsibility for taking the action necessary for him or herself to achieve the overall goal.

3   At a convenient point, collect in the questions and stick them onto a beach ball or other (classroom-appropriate!) inflatable. Alternatively, you can pass the Wonderball randomly around the classroom and allow learners to read out their question before sticking it on and passing it on. After a couple of minutes, once everyone feels their particular question is represented (there will be plenty of duplicates – just ask learners to request the Wonderball if they've not yet heard their question mentioned), you can collect the ball back in.

---

[1]   Isabella Wallace and Leah Kirkman, *Pimp Your Lesson! Prepare, Innovate, Motivate and Perfect* (London: Bloomsbury, 2014).

4   Consider the questions the learners have submitted – they will allow you to establish a general starting point as well as see what to focus on in the activity that follows. (Don't plough ahead with your original plans if these questions indicate that your plans were misjudged.)

5   Towards the end of the lesson (or series of lessons), allow the question-covered Wonderball to be passed randomly around the class. Each learner who catches it must remove one of the questions and attempt to answer it, or alternatively open up this question to the rest of the class. By this point, the learning that has occurred in the lesson (or series of lessons) should have enabled the learners to be able to answer the questions that they and their classmates posed before the learning journey began.

6   Bask in the glory of this visible progress and celebrate this achievement with your class. Showing your learners the undeniable progress they have made from one end of the lesson or unit of work to the other is a *very* powerful act.

An adaptation of this strategy is to write the kick-off questions yourself and attach them to the ball. If you're feeling really outstanding, and you have one of those packs of sticky notes that come in different colours, then you might like to differentiate your questions by colour. You can do this tactfully so that when Clever Clive catches the ball you can say, 'OK, Clive, I'd like you to pick … erm … a pink one please!' In this way, your assignment of questions to individuals looks arbitrary but in fact is cleverly and sensitively differentiated. Alternatively, you can tell learners that the questions are colour-coded according to difficulty/level/grade. In this way, every learner has the option of choosing a question that they feel is appropriate to their current target, as well as having an exciting opportunity to really challenge themselves.

There are many more practical and engaging ways to allow you to establish the starting point of your learners. Here are a few of our favourites.

Strategy: Boarding Card/Landing Card

This is a cute and quirky little trick to frame your lessons and consolidate learning. Imagine, for a moment, that your lessons are as exhilarating – and cover as much ground – as an international flight.

In this scenario, your lesson is a first-class trip on a top class airline. Provide each learner with a 'boarding card' as they enter the classroom. (This can be a very simple template – it only needs to say 'boarding card' and provide a space for the learner to write.) Don't keep them queuing to get in – none of your budget airline hell-on-earth here. Whisk them in with your best steward/stewardess manner and get them seated for the trip of a lifetime. You can either instruct learners to write down on their boarding card key learning points from the previous lesson, or ask them to note down one thing that they are wondering about today's topic. The boarding card provides an immediate 'hook' to capture learners' interest from the outset. It is also great for immediately engaging early-arrivers while you wait for passengers who are, quite frankly, cutting it a little fine …

I bet you can guess where we're going with the 'landing card'. For those of you who've never had the adventure of travelling to a country where you are required to complete a landing card (or arrival card), this is the document that flight attendants hand out about three-quarters of the way through your flight (or earlier to kill time!) on which you fill in details about the purpose of your trip. Distribute your simulated landing cards at around about the same point during your lesson, so that learners have the final quarter of the lesson to be thinking about what they can write on it. Before the close of the lesson, ask learners to note on their landing card either the key concepts, facts or skills that they have learnt in this lesson, an evaluation of their own work/effort or one thing that they would like to investigate further. This task can be issued for homework if appropriate.

To be really clever (and save paper too) you can design these cards so that the boarding and landing passes are on either side of the same card. In this way, you can redistribute the boarding cards – after you have scrutinised them – and learners can then ensure that the landing comments they write at the end of the lesson correspond to the boarding comments they wrote at the beginning.

Both the boarding and landing cards enable you to access essential information about prior learning, existing knowledge and areas of confusion. Whether you consult the cards during or after the lesson, they provide an excellent tool for informing future planning.

Disclaimer: while we are endorsing teacher-in-role and fun in the classroom, we do not advise a sudden change of career. Nor do we accept any responsibility should teachers begin leaving classrooms in droves to discover their inner flight attendant.

Boarding Card

The 3 key things I learnt last lesson:

_____

_____

_____

What I need to find out/learn to do this lesson:

_____

_____

_____

Landing Card

The 3 key things I learnt this lesson:

_____

_____

_____

What I need to find out/am still unsure about:

_____

_____

_____

Strategy: The Walking Chocolate Bar

We all know that the perfect bar of chocolate has at least eight squares. With this in mind, give each learner a piece of paper and ask them to fold it neatly into eight sections. (There may not be any actual chocolate involved in this activity – sorry – but there is a little cross-curricular numeracy!) Once learners have their eight squares in hand, they must circulate in the classroom, finding eight separate people who can tell them eight different things or original ideas about the topic. Each time the learner gains a new idea or piece of information, they must write it down in one of the eight squares (in their own words) to show that they have listened and understood. It usually only takes a couple of minutes for them to fill in all eight squares, at which point you can draw the class back together.

One of the great things about this activity is that even those learners who are initially stuck can begin to share the ideas that they accumulate from other learners. You may well notice a number of other exciting phenomena too:

- Learners who initially assess themselves as knowing nothing about the topic often discover that they actually know several things – once these are teased out by the activity.

- Learners who already consider themselves experts in this topic usually discover something new or are reminded of something they had completely forgotten.

- As learners attempt to find a nugget of information or an idea that the other learner has not yet collected, they find themselves talking through the whole range of facts or ideas that they are accumulating.

- New learning gets reinforced as it is repeated and spread around the class.

- The class gradually reaches a more common understanding without you needing to do any talking.

When you decide to end the activity, bring the learners back together and then collate ideas and information as a class. You should find during the collating stage that not only can you correct any misconceptions, but each learner's eight squares will probably turn into sixteen! Learners should already have made some progress through the assembling of additional ideas, and you will have ascertained a general feel for current levels of understanding in your class.

Try This ...

Each learner should now have at least eight different ideas or pieces of information. Ask them to include all of these in the piece of work that follows this initial task.

Strategy: Prior Knowledge Questionnaires

Questionnaires are simple but useful. This task involves issuing learners with a series of key questions related to the topic you will be covering in the following lesson. After collecting in the learners' responses at the end of the previous lesson, you can review these to determine current levels of understanding in your class and use this information to inform your planning for the subsequent lesson. Be sure to let your learners know that this exercise is simply designed to let you ascertain their levels of understanding. It is not a test!

Remember to be a chameleon teacher. If you discover that many of the learners already know far more than you thought they would at this stage, don't plough ahead with tomorrow's lesson plan regardless. If you do, progress is likely to be minimal or even non-existent. Similarly, if their prior knowledge is inferior to what you had anticipated, you'll need to adjust your plans accordingly.

Strategy: What I Know (from A to Z)

We're sure you won't be a stranger to the fact that when some learners are asked what they know about something, their default response is often 'not much' or 'nothing'. This usually comes down to a lack of self-confidence in themselves as a learner. Of course, the likelihood is they do have *some* frame of reference when it comes to most topics, so the trick is to tease out this information. This activity is a great way to extract information that learners didn't even acknowledge they had.

Learners can work as individuals, pairs or in groups. Ask them to write the letters of the alphabet down their page and then consider the given topic carefully. Their task is then to think of at least one topic-related word or phrase that begins with each of the letters.

An element of competition can be particularly helpful in drawing out hidden knowledge, and a time limit will help learners to think very hard and dig deep for those revelatory moments!

Try This ...

At the end of the lesson, partway through or for homework, ask learners to add to their A to Z list. If they have acquired new knowledge or understanding, they should be able to add additional words or phrases to their original list. Ask them to make these additions in a different colour pen so that you, and they, can clearly see what gains have been made over the course of the lesson.

Beware of Traffic Light Signals

As chameleon teachers, one of our superpowers is having encyclopaedic-like knowledge of our learners, and being able to use strategies that allow us to ascertain levels of understanding and skill quickly and effectively when necessary. Sometimes, however, we may feel that it's really useful to get an idea from the learners themselves about where they honestly *feel* they are in terms of their understanding. Encouraging learners to establish in their own minds where they feel they currently are in terms of understanding, knowledge or skill is a powerful, metacognitive activity. It forces learners to consider what they need to focus on and why, as well as flagging up for them the opportunity they are about to be given to make measurable progress.

Now, this is absolutely fine as long as we don't confuse it with an accurate, *expert* assessment of their knowledge, skill or understanding. To appreciate the important distinction we are making here, it is useful to consider the popularly used strategy, 'thumbs up, thumbs down'. This is a practice which involves learners signalling to the teacher whether they understand a concept by pointing their thumbs upwards to indicate they understand, downwards to indicate they 'don't get it' and horizontally to indicate they're 'not sure'.

It is clear that, at best, this strategy will only give us an indication of the learners' *perception* of their own understanding. Their self-assessment may, of course, be completely wrong. For example, they may mistakenly believe that they have not understood when actually their work demonstrates a high level of aptitude, or they may incorrectly believe that they have understood but in fact have totally misinterpreted instructions or concepts. At worst, 'thumbs up, thumbs down' will simply have learners conforming to the majority stance. After all, who among us would be happy to be the downwards thumb-pointer when all around us thumbs are pointing skywards?

The same applies to traffic light systems which are used in a similar way. If a learner displays a green card, you may well be getting some useful information regarding how confident they *feel* about their work, but you cannot confuse this with your own expert assessment of what they can actually *do*. It would be extremely unwise of us to see before us a sea of thumbs up or green cards and think, 'Great, they've got it! Let's move on!'

> **You can use 'traffic light signals', 'thumbs up, thumbs down' or 'rate your state on a progress line' to gauge levels of learners' confidence, but these self-assessment strategies should never be relied on as an accurate, expert assessment of genuine understanding and knowledge.**

However, there is a very effective alternative use for traffic light signals in your classroom, and one that will support you greatly in your mission as a chameleon teacher. Rather than learners holding up green or red objects to indicate what they perceive to be their understanding of a concept, the objects are placed on desks during group or individual work to signal to the teacher whether they are getting on just fine and don't currently want any assistance (green object), or completely confused and need to ask some questions before they go any further (red object).

In this scenario, you can use your swively chameleon teacher eyes to spot any flashes of red on display around the classroom and offer targeted guidance in a timely manner. This use of traffic lights is not only infinitely more discreet, it also fosters a culture of learners taking responsibility for their own progress. Nevermore will they have the excuse that the reason they're still sitting in front of a blank page and chatting with their friend is because they 'didn't get it' – because, in that case, they should have had their red signal on display!

Strategy: Assume Your Starting Position

We don't wish to underrate the value of self-assessment in the classroom, so the following activity is an effective strategy for gauging confidence levels and getting information about where learners currently perceive themselves to be at any point in the topic.

Place descriptors for different levels of understanding at various posts around the classroom. For example, one post might read, 'I think I know how to add using the number line, but I'm still a bit unclear about how to use the blank number line and the TUB [Tens, Units, Both] method,' while another post might read, 'I think I understand how to use the number line, the blank number line, the TUB method and the number square,' and so on.

You're going to ask learners to go and sit at the post that they feel best reflects their current understanding. But before you ask them to do this, allow them to scrutinise their exercise books and circulate to read the descriptors very carefully.

Once learners have gathered in groups at their chosen posts, your classroom will have been automatically organised in such a way that you are now in a prime position to ensure each group can receive the precise support they feel they require in order to make progress.

But don't forget the proviso above: what you're getting here is information about how the learners *perceive* they're doing. While this is valuable information in itself, you should still use your own assessment to support individuals appropriately as new progress is made or gaps are discovered. You should also bear in mind that this perception of their confidence with a topic may change once they begin the actual task – it is entirely possible that they will have underestimated or overestimated their understanding, so mobility between groups should be encouraged.

Why Teaching Assistants are Priceless

With the careful monitoring and frequent evaluation of learners' gains and understanding being so singularly important to great teaching, it is clear to see just how invaluable an extra adult in the room can be. That additional pair of discerning eyes can play a very important role in ascertaining levels of understanding, engagement and progress. If this esteemed colleague knows what they're looking for, they can spot learners' misconceptions that you may have missed, eureka moments that may have gone unnoticed or pockets of learners who are struggling to keep up, and they can feed back this valuable information to you so that you can be an even more skilful chameleon teacher.

The following is a list of practical things you can do to empower your teaching assistant, or other adult helper, to help you be the ultimate chameleon teacher.

■ Make sure your teaching assistant knows the following four things:

1 Where you feel learners currently are in terms of their understanding and skill.

2 What you are hoping learners will be better at by the end of the lesson.

3 What you will need to see the learners doing in order to know for sure that they've achieved the lesson objective.

4 What activity you have planned to enable the learners to meet the objective and demonstrate their understanding.

(For a more in-depth explanation of these crucial elements of your planning, see Chapter 3.)

■ Be especially aware of the importance of the third point above: your teaching assistant needs to be clear about what, specifically, will indicate that a learner has achieved the objective. And so do you and the learners, because otherwise the learners will only get there and win your approval by pure chance! See Chapter 3 for some examples of what this might look like.

■ Ask your teaching assistant to gather the questions that learners have as they are working. They might, for example, circulate with a notepad and pen, asking questions like, 'What are you wondering as you do this?', 'What part of this are you finding most difficult?' or 'What would you like some more help with?' This valuable information can be brought back to you so that you can use it to inform your subsequent teaching. (See Chapter 5 for more ideas on this technique and the Wonderwall.)

■ Ask your teaching assistant to circulate around the classroom, taking care to ascertain who is 'getting it', who isn't and who is finding it too easy. Ask them to try and get an idea of which learners are engaged in the task and those who are struggling to remain focused. If possible, ask them to make written notes for you to reflect on after the lesson. All of this precious information can be relayed back to you. In essence, your teaching assistant can help you to assess the impact of your teaching as you teach. Only in very specific circumstances should your teaching assistant be seated in one location with only one child throughout an entire lesson. You would never spend an entire lesson sat in one location, so you should not expect your teaching assistant to either.

- If possible, provide your teaching assistant with at least one good example of the kind of work you are hoping to see from your learners. If relevant, it should include clear workings, explanations and annotations.

- If you are working on an extended writing piece, provide your teaching assistant with appropriate sentence stems or phrases to get ideas going for learners who may be stuck or slow to get started on the task.

- Make sure that your teaching assistant knows your classroom routines, especially those pertaining to self-reliance and learner responsibility. Are you happy for learners to be provided with the 'answer'? Do you use routines such as 3B4Me or the 4Bs (Brain, Book, Buddy, Boss) (described in Jim Smith's *The Lazy Teacher's Handbook*[2] and elsewhere; see also Chapter 7)? Are learners permitted to get up and help themselves to resources to assist them or do they need to ask permission? Have you got an Enable Table (see Chapter 7) where learners can go to get additional information?

Being a chameleon teacher means remaining constantly aware of the importance of getting feedback from our learners about their understanding, so that we can intervene, support, challenge and adapt where necessary. Because of the never-ending nature of this mission, we can sometimes be a bit unimaginative about the format in which we get learners to give their feedback. Sometimes we might ask learners to produce a piece of writing to demonstrate what they know, which means we won't discover areas of confusion until we take in the books to mark. More often than not, we will 'check understanding' simply by posing questions to the whole class and getting answers to them from a minority of learners. It is useful to remember that while these might be our default methods, there are other ways to get crucial feedback from our learners – *all* our learners (not just a few of them) – about what they're understanding and where they're not quite hitting the mark. In the next chapter, you'll find a whole host of strategies that will allow you to get immediate visible feedback from every learner in the class.

---

[2] Jim Smith, *The Lazy Teacher's Handbook: How Your Students Learn More When You Teach Less* (Carmarthen: Crown House Publishing, 2010).

Chapter 2

Undeniable Progress

Practice That Eliminates Passengers

No Passengers Allowed!

With the best will in the world, it is difficult to avoid teaching to the loudest learners in our class. Sometimes they are literally loud because they are a serial disturber of the peace – with their voice as the nefarious weapon. Sometimes they are physically loud because they fidget, fuss, turn around and move about the classroom uninvited. Even when they are literally loud – consistently providing ideas, responses and thoughts to the questions you raise – they belong to the category of learners who can dominate our attention, both positively and negatively. The progress that these learners are making (or not making) is quite clear to us over the course of a lesson.

The learners who require more astute observation are the *invisible learners*: the ones who come into our lessons, cause no fuss or conflict, and are skilled at coasting under our radars, eclipsed by the huge range of loud peers around them. Not out of any malice or trickery, these invisible learners are able to avoid the confrontation of being accountable for their participation in lessons by being manifestly compliant – their exercise books are out, their pens are poised and eye contact is being made – so you are unaware they have made little or no progress until the books are taken in and the misunderstandings and/or lack of productive work becomes all too visible. Although it can be acted upon and rectified retrospectively, in many ways it is already too late.

> **Invisible learners find out that they can get away with not being involved in learning, which they perhaps find difficult, boring or are maybe even too under-confident to participate in, by sheer virtue of being inoffensively passive.**

The underperformance of invisible learners due to their lack of engagement is just as concerning as the lack of progress from learners who prevent their own advancement through disruption: it is an undesirable learning behaviour that prevents them from making gains in their knowledge, skills and understanding. One way that we can combat this, and ensure that these learners make good progress and do not opt out of their learning, is to plan activities that 'force' participation from all. Planning activities that make non-participation obvious means that it is much easier to spot the struggling learner, offer them support and draw them into activities before they have a chance to fall behind.

The other advantage of using strategies that force participation is that the progress in your lesson becomes highly visible. This is obviously desirable for the class teacher – who can then react and respond to the learning accordingly. But the class teacher is not the only stakeholder for progress in the classroom. Ensuring that progress is visible to the learners in the class, and flagging this up, is motivating and empowering for those at the crux of the learning. Though the gains, certainly over just one lesson or even a portion of a lesson, may be small, spotting them and celebrating them is a sure-fire way to ensure that the class remain keen to continue moving forward. Failing to see the point of a learning activity is the quickest way to switch learners off, especially the more reluctant learners in the group. By demonstrating to them the gains that are being made in the short term, the purpose of their learning will be much clearer. Making progress highly visible is also no bad thing for any other visitor who may find their way into your classroom, be it an internal or external observer, who will likely have their pen poised to note whether learners are making gains in the lesson!

What About the Angry Birds?

Setting our learners free from the shackles of passive learning and building in opportunities for *all* learners to be active participants in the development of knowledge, skills and understanding is an empowering shift in the classroom. Not only will the reluctant, or invisible, learners be drawn into their learning as you plan activities that demand active participation from all, but your existing loud learners will also have purposeful ways to shine.

By building in active participation, you will be setting your little birds free to actually *do* something with their learning rather than just absorb it. Unfortunately, our little birds can be a suspicious breed, so when we shift our professional practice, rather than being met with enthusiasm that matches our own, we can be greeted instead by 'angry birds': learners who would prefer to act within the confines of the learning habits they have been used to. They may be frustrated that they are no longer permitted to 'hide' and be passive in the lesson.

Learners may feel exasperated when you begin to introduce more activities that place greater demands on them discovering and practising, rather than just being told. It is important to remember that when we begin to approach our teaching in a different way, even if it is a slight shift, it is not only ourselves that need to be re-trained in our habits, but also our learners. It will take practice and persistence to get them to fully embrace a more learner-led environment, but rest assured that the persistence will be well worth the outcome.

Consider some of the following practical strategies as ways to eliminate the 'passengers' in your lessons and build the ethos of active participation.

Strategy: The Vertical Relay (The Only Way Is Up!)

The vertical relay is a collaborative exercise where learners work together as a team to complete a task with in-built levels of increasing challenge. The class is divided into teams and a stimulus (ideally produced on a large piece of paper) is provided to each team. This can be pinned up around the walls of the room or, if wall space is scarce, simply placed in the centre of a group of tables. Each member of the team, in turn, contributes to the group task before passing on the 'baton' (in this case, a pen) and then joining the back of the queue again. You'll find that a lot of peer teaching occurs as learners confer with and support each other throughout the process, ensuring that each member of the team is contributing to the end product.

To track individual contributions and ensure that all team members are participating, assign a different coloured pen to each learner. To ensure that the ideas can be attributed entirely to the learner in question – and not just being fed to them by other team members – you can always run a 'silent relay' where learners can only encourage each other through body language and facial expressions.

The 'vertical' part of the relay is ensuring that there are varying levels of challenge available in completing the task, and providing higher points value to higher-level responses. In this way, no learner is capped and everyone can attempt to gain the greatest number of points for their team by pushing themselves to the next level of challenge. For example, in a history lesson where learners are demonstrating their understanding of political alliances at the start of the Second World War, the team could be presented with a blank map to fill in. They could earn one point by labelling a country and correctly indicating their political alliance, two points for identifying a key political figure from that country and three points for explaining how they came into the war.

The collaboration and competitive environment is motivating and allows learners to support and stretch one another. Implementing the rule that each person can use their turn to either provide a new idea or add to/correct an idea that is already there, ensures that learners are not only focused on adding their own contributions, but also on evaluating those of their teammates as they go along.

Another excellent way to get learners to take in others' ideas is to allow a timed 'magpie', where they get a short burst of time (e.g. 30 or 60 seconds) to go around the class and 'steal' any ideas they had not thought of to record on their own sheets (see Chapter 4 for more on this). Although the class feels like this is a deliciously sneaky cheat and an exciting way to rack up points, they are, in fact, simply picking up best practice from their peers and expanding their own understanding.

You can use the Vertical Relay to establish a baseline with your class. It's a quick and highly visible way to verify what your learners know at the outset of a lesson. You can also use this strategy as a way to check progress at intervals throughout the lesson as the teams add to, or correct, their initial responses.

Try This ...

Use the Vertical Relay for:

Task	1 Point	2 Points	3 Points
Label a diagram, map or image	Label a key part	Label a detail	Add information
Highlight and annotate a piece of text for specific textual features (guided reading)	Identify and highlight a particular feature	Correctly label the feature	Explain the effect or purpose of the feature
Develop collaborative mind maps to collect ideas or to plan. (This can be an excellent alternative to the whole-class collation of ideas that we often create at the front of the room but which only provide insight into the thoughts and opinions of a fraction of the class)	Contribute an idea	Build on someone else's idea	Suggest an alternative
Brainstorm ideas for an exam question	Contribute an idea	Provide evidence for an idea	Explain why an idea is relevant
Fill in the answers to sums	The bottom row	The middle row	The top row (the most challenging)

Task	1 Point	2 Points	3 Points
Spot the mistakes – a punctuation relay is a great example of this. The team is given a piece of writing with all punctuation and capital letters removed, so learners need to add one piece of punctuation on each turn	A capital letter or full stop correctly placed	A comma, question mark, exclamation mark or speech marks correctly placed	Apostrophes, semicolons and brackets correctly placed
Contribute one word each in turn – without conferring. Learners have to continually adjust where they thought the sentence was heading, and are therefore obliged to play close attention to sentence-level features	Correct sentencing	Interesting vocabulary	Figurative language

Strategy : Crash! Bang! Wallop!

This strategy is a highly visible way to establish, in a short period of time, your learners' understanding of a given concept. As with Vertical Relay, you can use this to very quickly ascertain the starting points of your class, and as a means to assess progress against the learning objective. It is a quick and easy way to assess the impact of your teaching so that you know whether learners are ready to move on to the next stage of the lesson.

Crash! Bang! Wallop! involves learners providing a physical signal when they can recognise an aspect of their learning aurally or visually. For example, in a maths lesson where you wish to teach (or perhaps remind) the class about the 8 times table, display a 1–100 square on the board and begin counting together as a class. When counting, learners must provide a physical signal, like putting up their hand or bending their knees (if they are standing) when they see and/or hear a number that they know is a multiple of 8 – thus showing that they have recognised it.

As a baseline-setting activity, there can be no clearer way for you, or your class, to illustrate that they require some input on their 8 times table than seeing their classmates bobbing or waving out of unison. Repeat the exercise after some input and practice and, if suitable progress has been made, you and the learners will see the chosen physical signal happening in harmony. In the event that there are still some in the class who are a bit woolly on the concept, you will quickly be able to spot them and offer appropriate support and intervention. Of course, it is likely that there will be some learners who are unsure about the concept and start off by watching what their classmates are doing. However, take heart, because as these nervous learners observe and copy their classmates, they will undoubtedly amass new understanding.

You can increase the challenge of the activity by providing more than one feature for learners to 'spot'. In the numeracy example above, you may also wish to have learners looking for multiples of another number – for example, they should bend their knees when they see and hear a multiple of 8 and put their hand up when hear a multiple of 6.

Not only will you get immediate, visible feedback about whether your class has successfully grasped the concept you've been teaching them, and about whether it's safe to move on, but you will also be able to identify misconceptions on the spot.

This strategy is extremely versatile. For example, you can:

- Provide true and false statements about the topic and let learners provide a physical signal to indicate which statements they believe are correct .

- Display a piece of work and, as you read it aloud, ask learners to indicate wherever the piece meets a particular success criteria.

- Display a piece of work and, as you read it aloud, ask learners to indicate where the mistakes are.

- Display a series of images or words and let learners indicate which is an example of the topic they have been learning about.

Try This ...

Ask learners to watch closely for key features in a film clip. Often learners will dutifully watch a given clip but will treat that time as a bit of a break or a relaxation opportunity and, mouths agape, will allow the clip to wash over them. By asking them to look out for certain key features, active participation is required and they will be accountable for seeking out the important aspects you have asked them to spot. Rather than the teacher acting as interpreter and highlighting all the key features for them, it is the learners who are called upon to observe these features for themselves.

Strategy: Habit Spotter

Teachers only have one pair of eyes (contrary to rumours about the ones in the back of our heads!) and, with 30 learners in a class, it's impossible to make every one of them feel as if we are aware of their learning behaviour at every moment throughout the lesson. Consequently, learners who want to take a back seat, not give it their best or to opt out altogether will seize opportunities where they can do this discreetly, away from watchful eyes. Habit Spotter is a wonderful solution to this issue as it raises a learner's self-awareness throughout the lesson – not just when the teacher is addressing them as an individual.

First, decide what 'habit' it is that you most want to foster in your learners. This might be linked to your school's common values or it might be a special target for your particular class (e.g. perseverance, independence, sharing ideas, trying hard, listening carefully). We often bandy terms like this around and tell learners that we want to see them exhibited, but sometimes we forget to be explicit about what these habits look like in practice in the classroom. As a result, they can easily become vague goals, devoid of success criteria and with ambiguous meanings. Habit Spotter raises learners' understanding of what these behaviours look like in reality.

Next, issue each individual in the class with the name of another class member on whom they are secretly assigned to spy for the duration of the lesson. Their mission is to keep a lookout for their designated classmate exhibiting the habit you have indicated. When they observe their 'spottee' displaying the habit, they should make a quick note about what they saw. At this point, they can declare 'Spotted!' (or something similar) and you can ask them to share what they have observed so you can celebrate the great learning behaviours demonstrated.

It may be that you want learners to look out for several important habits, in which case, a card like the one featured below can be extremely useful.

You are the *Habit Spotter* for

Catch them displaying a habit, jot down some brief details and declare 'Bingo!' when they've exhibited them all!

Embrace challenge	Try hard
Creatively adapt	Persevere

Why does this strategy help to eliminate passengers in your classroom? First, it emphasises that, above all else, *learning behaviour*, *attitude* and *mindset* are the things that will make the most significant difference to a learner's progress. Second, the knowledge that they are being closely observed at all points in the lesson makes learners more aware of any automatic tendency they might have to coast or rely on other people to work for them. Third, there is something extremely liberating about knowing that for once, in this class full of 29 other people, someone somewhere will be noticing, acknowledging and appreciating everything they do!

Strategy: Catch a Habit

This is an endearing adaptation of Habit Spotter, and one that is especially suitable for little 'uns. To really emphasise the importance of active participation and good learning habits in your classroom, display a labelled container for each of the habits you want the learners to exhibit. Children should be regularly reminded to look out for examples of the habits being exhibited by anyone in the classroom. When they 'catch' someone demonstrating one of the habits, they can let either the teacher or teaching assistant know so that a note can be written about the child who has displayed the habit and placed in the correct container. Alternatively, the child can write the note themselves, including the name of the child they spotted, and place it in the appropriate jar.

You can choose how you use these notes subsequently. You might decide to read them all out at the end of a lesson and celebrate these examples of great learning behaviour, or you could simply reward the relevant youngsters with a postcard home. The children will become far more aware of the nature of their interactions with other people if they know that they will receive praise for showing certain habits.

Strategy: The Mexican Wave (of Voices)

When utilising whole-class questioning, it can be very difficult to obtain a response from each individual learner. This provides a perfect opportunity for reluctant learners to switch off, or for learners to become disengaged in the thinking process because their idea is not given airtime. The verbal Mexican Wave is a great way to give everyone a chance to voice an idea, and for you to quickly ascertain how *all* learners have responded to a thinking question.

After posing a question and providing some thinking time, begin on one side of the classroom and start the wave of voices. As you gesture across the class, learners should verbalise one key idea that they have in response to the question that has been posed. Wait until you have made it all the way across the classroom before offering any feedback on the ideas that you hear. Very quickly you will be able to gather what the key ideas, and perhaps misconceptions, are in relation to your question and can debrief accordingly. The 'wave' can also be used as a great discussion tool, by asking learners to share which ideas stood out for them, or were most interesting.

Strategy: Show What You Know

It is important to remember that not every technique we employ to make participation mandatory needs to be a whizzy one. Show What You Know is a prime example of a simple yet effective way to glean what all learners have understood about a question you have posed. Using mini-whiteboards so that learners can record and show, en masse, their answer to a question is a quick way for you to see responses from all learners. Misconceptions can be identified and corrected, interesting perceptions can be picked out and developed and, once again, any learner who has chosen to opt out can be quickly identified and drawn back into the learning process. Remember that asking learners to record and display their response on a mini-whiteboard is very different to simply asking them to indicate whether they think they've understood or not.

Strategy: What He/She Said!

Using talk-partners can be an effective way to give all learners an opportunity to voice their thinking in response to whole-class questioning. Develop an ethos of 'listening to each other' by posing a question to the whole class and then asking learners to share their own ideas with a partner before you choose a selection of learners to report back on *their partner's* ideas. This will prevent learners from just hopping onto their soap box to announce their own ideas and then subsequently just nodding and smiling absently when it is their partner's turn to share. With the possibility of having to report back on another's thoughts, learners will be forced to engage with their partner's ideas as well as sharing their own in a clear and thoughtful way.

Group Work Is No Place to Hide

Providing opportunities for learners to work together and learn from one another is an important part of an authentic learning experience – being able to collaborate effectively is one of the most useful skills we can equip our learners with for life outside the classroom. It is important to note, however, that simply presenting the opportunity to work together does not necessarily facilitate meaningful progress or learning, any more than

buying a gym pass automatically facilitates meaningful weight loss or improved fitness. Consider these hard truths about group work in your lessons:

- Group work *can* be a place to conceal bad behaviour. Because you are consenting to a noisy classroom environment, any off-task behaviour can go undetected.

- It is impossible to track the exact contributions of every class member during group-work sessions.

- The more confident, or more able, learners can mask a lack of understanding or productivity in their weaker or less confident classmates.

This is not to suggest that group work should be avoided. On the contrary, group work can be a great place to boost the confidence of reluctant learners, as they have a more focused and legitimate opportunity to be supported by their peers. Group work is a means to give a voice to *all* your learners. A whole-class discussion only provides opportunity for a fraction of the class to weigh in on a topic or question, as it is difficult to take feedback from everyone in a timely fashion. Group work gives all learners ample opportunity for their voices and ideas to be heard and allows them to build on and respond to their peers' ideas.

So, how do you know that they are *all* using this brilliant opportunity and not just sitting back and enjoying the ride? Try the following strategy to make participation in group work visible.

Strategy: The String Thing

This is a wonderful antidote to the uncertainty surrounding who is contributing what to a group discussion, and a brilliant way for you, and the learners, to 'track' debate contributions within their groups.

You'll need a few balls of string for this – an inexpensive item which you can often find at pound shops in bags of three or four. Each small group is given a ball of string. When the discussion time starts, the first learner to contribute will pick up the string and keep hold of the end. The next learner to chip in on the discussion will take the ball from the previous person, keep hold of the length of string and pass the ball on to the next person who wants to say something and so on. This clever little technique results in an intricate web of string, mapped diagonally back and forth across the group, tracking the debate as it has unfolded between the learners.

This strategy has numerous benefits. First, from our point of view as teachers, we can circulate and ascertain very quickly which groups are getting stuck in with lots of ideas being shared, which groups are taking longer to get started or are struggling for ideas, and which individual learners have not yet contributed and which are dominating the discussion. The string indicates subtleties in approaches to group talk. For example, you'll find that while the string in most groups will zigzag in a freestyle fashion, you'll get the occasional group that systematically passes the string round in a circle, forcing ordered participation which is far less natural. These are great enlightening moments which can be used to discuss speaking and listening skills and group dynamics with your class. Ask learners to analyse the 'webs' they produce to see what that can tell us about their own discussion behaviour and that of their group. For instance, it is usually possible to identify where an intense exchange between two people has occurred (often indicating a disagreement of some kind) or where one learner has acted as a chairperson.

The other great thing the String Thing does is to encourage participation from learners who usually get away with taking a back seat in group work. While it is relatively easy for one person's lack of contribution to go unnoticed in a typical group discussion, it is far harder to opt out of contributing when the web of string visibly bypasses one individual. The string also significantly cuts down on interruptions, turns unruly arguments into orderly debate and encourages polite listening. It makes group discussion fun and interesting and it allows learners to analyse their own 'discussion behaviour'.

For more ideas on how to make participation in group work visible, see Talk Tokens, The Conch and The Silent Discussion in Chapter 4.

With the best multitasking will in the world, gathering feedback about our learners' development over the course of a lesson is virtually impossible with the sound of our own voices ringing in our ears. No matter how wise the pearl or sage the advice, the feedback we collect when teacher-talk takes over can only ever be superficial because it relies strictly on the way we interpret the learners' physical demeanour. Although body language and facial expressions can provide some indication of whether a learner is paying attention, interested, bored, happy, angry or confused, it can be just as easily misinterpreted or falsely represented. It is not unheard of for our learners, especially the serial passengers, to feign interest for the sake of an easy life. They know that if they nod and smile, or even just sit quietly and cooperatively, that it is less likely they will be caught out.

Ultimately, in planning opportunities for all learners to be making visible contributions to your lessons, an ethos of *learner-led talk* will develop. Once your learners are well-trained in purposeful, progress-oriented talk in lessons, it paves the way for you to well and truly cut down on the top-down dispersal of information and use your presence in the class to assess and monitor real progress, intervening only where it is most useful.

Progress in the classroom rarely happens by accident, and as we have seen already in this chapter, ensuring all learners actively engage is crucial for enabling progress for all. Of course, there are those golden moments where the proverbial penny drops when you least expect it, and where your learners take their learning in unexpected directions that surpass your expectations. As teachers we live for these moments – we relish and delight in them – but we shouldn't ever mistake them for the norm. Calculation, careful measurement and intuitive knowledge of our learners' abilities, knowledge and skills is at the core of ensuring that progress in our classrooms is visible and purposeful.

The passengers in our classrooms need special consideration to ensure that they, too, are drawn into the learning, so ensuring that there is nowhere for learners to hide in your lessons needs to be an important part of the planning process. None of these things can occur if we allow our talk to take over. Be sure to plan for the opportunities where *you* step back and enjoy the ride, taking in the scenery that is your learners' progress.

Chapter 3

What Makes a Great ...?

Success Criteria Made Simple

What makes a great birthday cake? This is a question that has plagued many seeking to utilise the inspiration they took from *The Great British Bake Off* to impress their friends and family. Imagine this scenario: an inspired cake-baker stays up until midnight preparing a great birthday cake for her 4-year-old son, fastidiously cutting out individual superhero emblems from fondant icing to adorn the cake he will share with his friends at his party the next day. She proudly produces the work of art, only to find that all the little critics immediately scrape the masterpieces off before tucking into the cake, and a healthy number stop to ask why there are no Smarties on top! The moral of the story is that this poor aspiring baker could have ensured greater success of her labours had she firmly established 'what makes a great birthday cake' from the perspective of a 4-year-old, rather than the Pinterest addicts she consulted instead.

This scenario, transposed to the classroom, can be even more heart-breaking for a learner. It calls to mind situations where learners proudly produce a piece of homework they have spent painstaking hours making *look* attractive with an illustrated cover-page, a border around the edges, impeccably word-processed (likely in a novelty font – Chiller, anyone?) and presented in a crisp plastic wallet, only to receive a lukewarm reception from their class teacher who was seeking more substance than style. From the teacher's perspective, it mirrors perfectly the experience of collecting in a set of exercise books following a lesson that you felt was well executed, believing the resultant work you set would be the perfect way to illustrate their progress and understanding, only to find that exercise book after exercise book suggests nearly the whole class didn't get it.

In both of these cases, the disappointing output cannot be blamed wholly on errant learners. The key to ensuring that learners give you what you want, and are illustrating their learning in a way that best facilitates progress and demonstrates their understanding, is to make the success criteria clear and accessible for all before embarking on the task. This is not new or revolutionary information; of course, in any context, an individual will do a better job if they are told explicitly how to do it every time.

This can be a point of frustration for teachers, especially when seeking to build more independent and resilient learners. Isn't the creative process inhibited if all the key 'ingredients' are pointed out for the learner? What about the aptitude of being able to choose the best skills and tools within a discipline to carry out a task or assignment effectively? Isn't this step in the process denied if the teacher is forever telling learners which techniques to use? Isn't 'success criteria' just a palatable way of saying 'spoon-feeding'?

In fact, there is a distinct difference between giving learners a step-by-step 'recipe' to completing a task and giving them clear guidance about your expectations. If your success criteria are more like a fill-in-the-blanks than a choose-your-own-adventure exercise, then the level of challenge you are creating in the task may need to be reconsidered .

That being said, in the early stages of acquiring a skill, sometimes the step-by-step recipe is necessary and desirable. This only becomes spoon-feeding when the skills are never progressed to a level such that the learners are expected to implement them independently of the teacher's recipe. Your success criteria should evolve as your learners' skills evolve. In due course, you will not need to spoon-feed the response learners give, but rather provide clear direction about appropriate features of their work.

Remember that providing success criteria need not be a top-down dictation of what your learners need to do in a given piece of work. This chapter will illustrate that, without using any Jedi mind-tricks or planting subliminal messages, the path to success can be communicated effectively without simply defaulting to teacher-led explanations.

Four-Steps for Progress-Oriented Planning

Clear, progress-oriented planning is the antidote to the hit-or-miss nature of the turn-up-and-talk approach to teaching. While it is possible to deliver a lesson that even that guy from *Dead Poets Society* would be envious of, good results from this method cannot be relied upon. With lecture-based teaching, it is extremely difficult to know whether the learners have sufficient skills and knowledge to effectively carry out the task you have planned. In fact, you may not discover their level of understanding until you take in the books and see the results.

None of the required groundwork happens by accident. At the heart of ensuring outstanding progress for every learner, there needs to be clear and calculated planning that takes each learner's individual needs into account. The impact of your teaching needs to be well-defined in order to ensure that the desired skills and knowledge are acquired over the course of the lesson. Consider the following four questions as your starting point for this progress-oriented planning.

What skills and knowledge do my learners already have that will support this task? What is the range of this baseline in the class?

What knowledge, skills and/or understanding do I want each learner to have acquired by the end of the lesson that they did not have at the beginning?

What will I need to see from each learner to know that they have achieved the learning objective?

What learning activities will be most effective in evidencing the knowledge, skills and/or understanding required to meet the learning objective?

Step 1: Establishing the Baseline

Chapter 1 outlined the importance of setting your baseline in ensuring the very best progress for your learners. It is this practice of establishing your learners' prior skills, knowledge and understanding that needs to be the first point of consideration in the progress-oriented planning process. From this informed position, you can ensure that you are pitching the challenge of your lesson effectively and differentiating accordingly. Taking into account the invariably different starting points of your learners is vital to begin considering the ways you will need to differentiate in order to ensure that there is opportunity for progress at all abilities and levels of understanding. Revisit this chapter for some practical strategies to assist in ascertaining that all-important baseline.

Step 2: Setting Learning Objectives with Real Purpose

The learning objective should never be a cursory exercise that is there to simply adorn the first slide of your PowerPoint or be dutifully copied at the top of each learner's page in their exercise book. The practice of writing the lesson objective at the beginning of each piece of work is poor proof that learners have understood it – all it proves is that they can copy a sentence. Likewise, it should not appear in your planning simply because there is a box for it in your departmental planning pro forma or scheme of work. Your learning objective should always be a very deliberate articulation of the knowledge, skills or understanding that you want your learners to have acquired by the end of your lesson.

The learning objective should also be sharply focused on what your learners will be able to do by the end of your lesson that they were not able to do beforehand (or what they will be more proficient at). Not every lesson you teach will be about new skills and information, so in these lessons that seek to review, revisit or develop existing skills and knowledge, you will need to ensure that there is room for progress and that it is not just an opportunity to repeat previously introduced skills. How are you up-skilling or refining the prior learning?

A mistake too often made in the planning process is deciding on the output, or what you want your learners to *do* in the lesson (e.g. 'Year 9 can make a comic strip today!'), without first considering the learning that you want to take place. If you want them to create a comic strip because you intend for them to understand the comic strip genre and the skill of creating comic books, then great. If the skill you are honing is identifying and distilling key events from a text, then brilliant – this could also be an apt output. However, if the comic strip has been chosen simply because it will engage the class or give them a chance to do something creative, then this needs some serious rethinking. Although engagement is an important part of the lessons we teach, it cannot be at the expense of meaningful learning. The output that we choose in a lesson should always be as a result of the skills we want the students to take away, not simply as a means to engage with some information.

While the acquisition of knowledge is naturally a desirable and worthwhile outcome from the lesson, it is unlikely that 'knowing' a set of information will be consistently sufficient in terms of meeting the rigorous demands of the curriculum and for challenging all learners. When considering the key learning you want to take place in your lessons, in both the short term and the long term, you must be cautious that you do not fall into the trap of having 'knowing' as the core learning that is taking place. If that old stalwart, Bloom's taxonomy, has taught us anything, it is that knowing something is at the very bottom of the heap in terms of challenge in learning. This is not to say that it is not valuable learning; it just needs careful consideration in terms of how learners will be able to challenge themselves in relation to the pursuit of it.

Step 3: Proof of Progress

Once you have established what learning you want to take place in your lesson, or series of lessons, it is important that you know what will be the clear markers of success and the best medium to observe them. For this part of the planning process you need to think carefully about what a 'perfect' example of the desired outcome would look like. What steps are involved in arriving at that perfect example, and how can you break these down and articulate them clearly for your learners?

Communication with your learners about markers of success is vital, so bear in mind the following things your learners should know about a task.

■ *The skills you are seeking to assess or that you are providing an opportunity to practise.*

This should be inherently linked to your lesson objective. Although learners may very well need to draw on a range of skills from the discipline in question, which are the key ones that you are looking for evidence of their proficiency in?

■ *The medium the work should be presented in.*

Is presentation paramount? Is there a specific format they should be using to record their work? Of course, we never want to invite intentional sloppiness in the presentation of work, but for formative pieces of work the thinking process is not always linear. Are markings and workings acceptable or is a more polished copy important?

Do you have a length or breadth in mind? This can be an incredibly frustrating question to be asked ('How many lines, Miss?') but it is a valid concern for learners. Do you simply want them to work to a time target rather than quantity? Is there a minimum expectation for the number of problems they solve or sentences they write? It can be limiting to enumerate your expectations too rigidly but you should aim to make your expectations clear.

◼ *The language or discourse they should use to be successful.*

Are you looking for specific terminology to be incorporated? Do you want them to include evidence or refer to any specific examples or sources? Is the complexity of their language choices important or is simplicity and clarity central for your task?

◼ *How the piece of work will be assessed.*

Are you using grades or levels? Is it a formative piece that will only be given diagnostic comments? Will the piece be chiefly peer-assessed or self-assessed? Are you using specific grading criteria (e.g. from an examination board)? If you already have a grading rubric prepared for the piece of work, it is usually useful to share this with your learners.

Setting clear success criteria is not solely for the benefit of the learners. The process of carefully determining the desired outcomes and what they will look like before setting the task, or even embarking on the teaching, is a great way to set expectations in your own mind and so direct your teaching with the end goal in mind.

Step 4: Choosing Activities That Best Suit the Intended Learning

After identifying where your learners are starting from, what you want them to learn and what that learning should look like, we finally get to the fun bit: choosing the learning activities that will best suit the knowledge, skills or understanding we want to develop. So, what are they actually going to *do* in the lesson?

These four steps will not only ensure that your lessons are planned with optimal progress in mind, but also that your learners will be well-equipped to be successful in the learning activities that you plan. At the core are clear expectations for your learners.

Sharing Success Criteria

The sharing of success criteria need not be flashy. The mechanism of sharing should be as clear as possible, always accessible to learners while they are undertaking the task and, ideally, should involve some active engagement on their part. Just as lectures are not always the most effective way for people to learn information, they are also not always the best method of explaining how best to approach a task.

Here are some strategies that will help you to involve your learners more in the process of making the criteria for success explicit.

Strategy: Checklist Challenge

Providing your success criteria to your learners in the form of a checklist to be used while they work can be a great way to keep the key ideas they need to include at the forefront while they are working. It can also be a useful reflective resource when learners assess their own work or return to it after assessment by someone else (teacher or peer). Include the lesson objective on the pre-printed resource to make it a clear record of the learning intentions in the lesson (and eliminate the potentially dull and time-consuming practice of copying out the learning objective!). Consider the following example from a Key Stage 3 English lesson:

Objective: To be able to use a range of persuasive devices in a formal letter	
Persuasive devices	Features of a formal letter
Use of hard evidence (facts)	Relevant addresses (sender and receiver
Use of soft evidence (opinions)	Salutation (apt for sender)
Rhetorical questions	Date

		Discourse markers
Rule of three		
Superlatives		
Figurative language (metaphor, simile, alliteration, etc.)		
Benefits		
Pre-empt possible criticisms		

Ongoing writing best practice

Correct paragraphing
End punctuation (. ? ! ...) – be cautious of long sentences
Mid-sentence punctuation (, ; : ...)
Capital letters
Spell-check (double-check homophones)

This example gives clear guidance about what learners should include in their piece of persuasive writing, but is by no means a step-by-step guide to completing the assignment. Learners have a reference point to guide their choices in the range of persuasive devices, but also have the freedom to include others that the class teacher has not put in the checklist. The checklist of ongoing writing best practice (which includes space for learners to personalise the areas of their writing that need refining) reminds learners about the other features of writing that their class teacher will take into account when assessing the piece of work.

A document like this, included alongside the piece of writing – be it in an exercise book or in an assessment portfolio – provides little doubt to any stakeholder in the work (e.g. learner, parent, manager) about what the most important features for a successful piece of work are. For the class teacher, this can focus anecdotal comments of praise and/or improvement when assessing the work. If the work is being word-processed, it works very well to have learners embed the table at the end to save time on photocopying and the guillotine.

A simple checklist is also a handy reference for your teaching assistant or any other adult helper you may have in the classroom. It will assist them in ensuring that they are emphasising the same skills and features that you are in a piece of work. Here are some examples:

Checklist for success: drawing a graph

- Graph is drawn on graph paper

- Pencil and ruler used to draw axes and line of best fit (if straight line of best fit)

- Scale on both axes goes up in equal amounts

- Axes labelled and units written in brackets

Checklist for success: badminton serve

- Extended arm stretched above head

- Racket faces forward

- Positioned at back of own court

- Shuttle travels to back of opponent's court

Strategy: Lost Property

This activity is a fun way of helping learners to identify and be able to articulate success criteria. It does require a set of resources but, as with most of the resource-based activities in this book, we implore you to have the learners generate these materials themselves. This plea isn't just because teachers are extremely busy. It's because when learners have created the resources themselves, they have a sort of instinctive buy-in to the success of the activity. They want the activity to go well because they have effectively written, directed and produced it.

The resources required for this task are suitcase-shaped pieces of paper or card with printed writing on each side. On one side will be the title of something that learners could be asked to produce, perform or write about (e.g. Instructions for Pet Care, A Pie Chart, A Map, A Children's Website, A Description of Your Family, An Essay About the Cold War, A Stir-Fry, A Free Kick). On the other side will be listed the ingredients that go into making a great example of this. So, if the item was 'An Effective Dance Routine', the other side of the card might read something like:

- Control
- Awareness of space
- Flexibility/suppleness
- Balance
- Reaction time
- Collaboration
- Precision
- Fluency
- Agility
- Coordination
- Timing

Once armed with a suitcase card each, learners must approach one another as if meeting in a lost property office, taking it in turns to play first the role of the lost property attendant and then the role of the poor soul who has mislaid their property. Both learners must keep the 'contents' on the backs of their cards secret at all times. Learner A looks at the item on the front of Learner B's card and identifies it as their lost briefcase. In order to convince the lost property attendant to release the briefcase to them, Learner A must describe the contents of the briefcase (the list on the back) correctly and in sufficient detail. If they successfully name the success criteria ingredients, then they win that suitcase to take away. If they are unable to list all the important contents, then the attendant *shows* them the full list but retains the suitcase. (The idea behind this is that next time the learner comes across that same suitcase, they should have a better chance of accurately naming the contents and therefore winning the card.)

Once the roles have been reversed (i.e. Learner A has played the role of the lost property attendant), learners will move on to repeat the process with other classmates. This means that during the game, at any one time, you will have some learners with a whole collection of suitcases, some with one or two and some with none at all. Remember that suitcases have to be handed over as soon as a classmate has correctly listed the contents, so they can be won and lost very quickly. If you want to bring in an element of competition and a sense of urgency, you can tell learners that the winner will be the person who is holding the most suitcases at the random point where you declare 'Stop!'

By requiring learners to articulate the success criteria for each of the tasks or skills, you are helping them to become explicitly aware of how to make progress and achieve to their highest potential. This activity works well with exam questions printed on the front of the suitcases and 'things you could mention in your answer' printed on the back. For much younger children, you can adapt this process with pictures – for example, a picture of a farm on the front of the suitcase and smaller pictures of the animals you might find on a farm on the back. Or a picture of a beach on the front and smaller pictures of things you might do on a beach on the back. Below are a number of cross-curricular examples of suitcases and their contents.

- They have basically three body parts i.e. head, thorax and abdomen
- They have no lungs
- They respire through their skin
- They live in colonies
- They lay eggs and not babies

Invertebrates

- Rhetorical questions
- Powerful words
- Repetition
- Address the reader
- Emotive language

Persuasive Writing

- Full title is present
- Pair of compasses has been used to draw neat circle
- Pencil has been used at all times
- Angles within each section of the pie chart correspond exactly to the proportions being illustrated

Drawing a Pie Chart

- A single melodic idea
- Continuous rhythmic drive
- Orchestral – strings, winds and harpsichord with very little percussion
- Abrupt shifts from loud to soft - achieved by adding or subtracting instruments
- A single musical piece intended to project a single mood or expression of feeling

Baroque Music

- A variety of colour
- A variety of texture
- Meat cooked through (if used)
- Vegetables still crunchy

Stir Fry

Strategy: The Great Race

This strategy solves a variety of age-old problems in the classroom:

- How do you model excellent work in a way which holds the concentrated attention of all learners?

- How do you carefully explain success criteria to learners so that they will remember them easily the next time they need to apply them in a piece of work?

- How do you tactfully differentiate when you have a wide range of abilities and starting points in your class?

- How do you turn any potentially dry and uninspiring task into something which is engaging and exciting for learners?

- How do you get learners working together in a controlled and focused way?

No, the heaven-sent solution we're about to offer is not recruiting Derren Brown to take the lesson! Instead, it's an exceptionally versatile and easy-to-implement classroom strategy.

To really reap the differentiation benefits of this technique, you will need to organise your class into ability groupings. In our opinion, this works best with groups made up of no more than four. Once the groupings are organised and ready to start the race, you can announce the first stage of the task to the class. As soon as a group feels they have successfully completed the initial stage (to a standard they are proud of) they send a runner to you to relay their handiwork. The runner might be required to show you, read to you or tell you something (this will depend on the task). To prevent learners from simply dashing through a task to find out what comes next, it is important that you make your floor standards clear from the outset so they know what you will expect as a minimum.

If you are pleased with what that particular grouping has produced, then you will *secretly* issue the next stage of the task to that runner, who will return to his or her group and begin work with their teammates once more. If you are not satisfied with what that particular group has produced then you can send them back to adapt and improve. Learners will quickly discover that it is not possible to sacrifice quality in favour of speed, and therefore will work together to generate the best response possible first time around. (For exam classes, this is a great way to get learners used to producing quality work under time constraints.)

Here's the deliciously clever bit: as a skilful chameleon teacher who is differentiating according to the varying needs of your learners, you can be far more discerning about what you accept from an especially able group. In fact (shhh, don't tell a soul!) you can easily and unobtrusively give completely different tasks to different groups. In other words, you can hold off forever-finish-firsters from completing the race before everyone else by challenging them with more and more difficult tasks, and you can support your least able groupings by giving them tasks which are especially tailored to their needs and carefully scaffold the work for them. Once your class is caught up in the excitement of the Great Race, you will see how easy it is to differentiate by task without the learners ever realising that they are working on diverse assignments.

So, why is the Great Race such a perfect choice for giving instructions and explaining the success criteria? Well, because it can be designed to directly answer that all-important question: 'What makes a great …?' Imagine that you wanted learners to understand how to complete a great piece of poetry analysis, and you wanted to model this for them in an engaging, precise and step-by-step manner. Let's say that there were eight key steps you wanted them to take in their critique – for example: (1) Write a sentence to explain what the poem first appears to be about; (2) Identify some examples of repetition and comment on their effect, and so on. By actually taking the learners through the experience of completing those steps one by one (rather than simply explaining the process to them through talk), they will be far more likely to be able to replicate the process when left to their own devices at a later date.

In effect, what you are doing with the Great Race is making absolutely explicit the precise steps that need to be taken, in the exact sequence, in order to produce a successful example of the task in hand.

What you think they're thinking . . .

What they're actually thinking . . .

Try This ...

The Great Race can be used:

- As an alternative to textbook work – give groups a text to read and release the textbook questions one at a time.

- To demonstrate the steps involved in answering a test question.

- To help learners craft sentence by sentence to compile a perfect paragraph.

- To help learners produce paragraph by paragraph to compile a perfect essay.

- To help learners tackle sum by sum or the stages involved in solving a mathematical problem.

- To take learners through a whole series of problems which would otherwise feel a daunting prospect.

- To help learners get better at locating information in a text while under pressure.

- To teach learners how to build a project or concept one step at a time.

- To help learners focus on the crafting language rather than just the content (e.g. 'Your next sentence must contain a simile').

Looking for Links (see Chapter 7) is another excellent strategy for getting learners to make explicit connections between success criteria, and what it looks like in practice, in an interactive way.

What Makes Great Learning Behaviour?

Sharing the definition of success should not be reserved exclusively for the discussion of individual projects and pieces of work. It should also include an explicit discussion about learning behaviours in your classroom. Great learning behaviours do not happen by accident – they are a result of ongoing high expectations and opportunities to be active in the learning process.

Good learning behaviour is different from the elements of what is considered to be 'good behaviour' in the traditional sense. It moves beyond sitting quietly and listening and putting your hand up at solicited moments. In the spirit of talk-less teaching, learning behaviour takes into account all the ways that learners are active in the acquisition of knowledge and skills. In what ways is their conduct in lessons supporting their progress? This might include being a skilled collaborator as a member of a group, supporting and taking advice from peers, utilising resources beyond the class teacher to help them when they are stuck – the definition is as flexible as the range of ages and subjects we teach.

You would not classify a learner who wants to show you their work at exasperatingly frequent intervals throughout its composition as badly behaved, but this habit is not a good learning behaviour. Similarly, you would not suggest that when a particularly able student takes over in a group-work situation (because they feel they can do it better than their peers) it is a display of poor behaviour. It is, however, an example of ineffective learning behaviour. Although conventionally 'good behaviour' certainly can facilitate good learning, the skills we are referring to as good *learning behaviour* are much broader.

So, how can we make this distinction for our learners and provide expectations about not only the quality of their work, but also about their conduct as learners? The following prompts may help to facilitate a guided conversation with your class about exactly what that might look like in your classroom:

■ What does participation look like in this class?

■ What do I do when I'm stuck?

■ What should my peers do for me in this class?

■ What should I do for my peers?

■ What equipment do I need to be successful in this class?

■ What does it mean/look like to 'work hard'?

■ How do I get feedback about what I'm learning?

We have already looked at two strategies that can help to facilitate a carefully guided peer-assessment of learners' participation (see Habit Spotter and Catch a Habit in Chapter 2). These call upon learners to observe specific, visible learning behaviours by their peers over the course of a lesson.

Clear Learning Objectives: The Path to Greatness

OK, so it may not be the path to 'greatness' in the larger sense, but clear learning objectives certainly pave the way for clarifying 'What makes a great …' for your learners. Learning objectives can feel like a particularly frustrating breed of administrative task, but they should never be seen as cursory.

There are a number of causes for teachers' frustration surrounding lesson objectives:

■ Every expert/local education authority adviser/consultant has a slightly different recipe for how they should be best articulated, and confusion and mixed messages naturally ensue.

■ The fine line between 'objectives' and 'outcomes' seems to overcomplicate the lesson planning process – and, anyway, aren't we supposed to be streamlining lesson planning?!

■ Sharing the learning objective can remove the element of 'surprise' in the lesson. Isn't this a bit like giving away the punch-line of a joke before the end?

■ Does the class even pay attention to the learning objective?

Your lesson objective – whether you call it an aim, a learning goal, a WALT (We Are Learning To) or some other clever acronym – should always be a sharp, simple articulation of the main direction of the learning your class will be doing over the course of your lesson. Learning should never be confused simply with a learning activity, which is usually evidence of the learning outcomes. A point to ponder: if you cannot pinpoint what your learners will be able to do by the end of your lesson that they could not do proficiently before they arrived, what was the point of the lesson? The gains made over one lesson may be small, but they should always be planned such that progress can be made, even if that progress is practice and refining.

With this in mind, your learning objective need not spoil the 'punch-line' of your lesson. The objective does not reveal content or 'give away' the key point; instead it informs your class what they will be able to do by the end of the lesson. If the main point of the lesson is to *know* or *understand* something, what skills will they have employed to gain that knowledge or understanding?

The burning question remains: does the class take any notice of the learning objective, or is it just a planning tool for the teacher? Furthermore, is it important for learners to know what the learning objective is? Ensuring that learners know where their learning is going *is* important: it allows them to understand why the lesson is unfolding in the way that it is, rather than just being along for the ride and seeing what their teacher asks them to do next.

Think about your sat-nav. When you begin a journey, you put in the postcode or location of where you are headed and wait for a route to be calculated. You begin the journey, follow the mild-mannered instructions given to you by the well-spoken sat-nav lady (or gentleman) and, voila! You end up at your desired end location. You haven't necessarily taken in how you got there as you were passively following directions, and the odds are that you wouldn't be able to replicate the journey at a later date without the help of the sat-nav. Your lesson objective and success criteria scaffold your lesson in a similar way to choosing to follow a map or finding out the directions ahead of time. When the learners can see what the end goal is, and the steps that they need to take to get there, the process will be more memorable and more meaningful.

Simply displaying the learning objective on the board at the outset of the lesson will likely not be the most effective way to ensure that your class takes notice of it. Although a record of the learning objective may be a useful reference point for future book scrutiny by parents, a manager or, indeed, the learners themselves, this need not be copied out by the learner. Consider alternative ways of keeping a record of this, such as printing the objective onto stickers for the learners to put on their work, publishing the day's objectives on the class website or blog or perhaps retrospectively giving them a copy of the week's objectives to stick at the back of their book for cross-referencing when needed. Facilitating a guided discussion about the objective at an early stage in the lesson will also make it much more likely that the learners will understand where their learning is heading that day.

Try some of the following strategies for helping your class to engage with the learning objective:

■ Learners assess their KWL of the objective – what they already *know*, what they *want* to know and, at the end of the lesson, what they've *learnt* (see Chapter 1).

■ Learners rank order the words in the learning objective in order of importance.

■ Create a toolbox of things the learners will need (prior and new learning) to achieve the learning objective.

■ Leave the verb out of the learning objective and provide learners with a list of learning verbs from Bloom's taxonomy. Decide as a group which is most appropriate.

■ Use a series of pictures to convey what your learning objective is and have learners decipher the objective from the images.

■ Provide a key word (or the topic) that the learning objective focuses on and have the class generate as many words as possible that link with the topic. After revealing the objective, reward the class if they achieve a pre-agreed threshold of words that are relevant to the learning.

■ Turn the learning objective into an anagram and have the class decode it correctly.

■ Ask learners to make links with prior learning. What objectives have they previously achieved that will help them to get started here?

■ Choreograph an interpretive dance to represent the learning objective. *Kidding!* (Although please let us know if you try this – and make sure you film it!)

■ Passing notes – have each learner in the class write down a question they may have about the learning objective and have them pass it around the room until you say 'Stop!' Each learner should then have one of their peers' questions and they should make it their task to have an answer for that question by the end of the lesson (see Chapter 5 for more details).

■ The Wonderball – as above, each learner should write down one question they have about the learning objective on a sticky note. The teacher gathers in the notes and sticks them onto a beach ball. At the end of the lesson, the ball is passed around the room and the 'catcher' attempts to answer the question (see Chapter 1 for more details).

- Edward de Bono's Six Thinking Hats[1] – pair up learners and assign each pair one of de Bono's hats. Pairs must assess the learning objective in light of the hat they are wearing. Debrief several ideas from each hat.

- Create an action plan with the class, complete with success criteria and possibly timings, about how the objective will be achieved.

- Show the learners the equipment they will require to achieve the learning objective (you may need to rely on images and metaphor here if the physical equipment required is not especially telling) and have the class work out what the objective is.

- Take the key words from the objective and play Taboo – conceal the words and describe them one at a time without using the word itself, or derivations of the word, until the class guesses correctly. Once they have discovered all the words, ask the class to create a learning objective.

Modelling a Great One

What better way to clearly illustrate success than by showing a clear example of what it looks like? Sometimes explaining just isn't enough and can become overly complex. Without an example to use as a guiding reference, learners often embark on a task unsure about exactly what their teacher is after. This is not to say that learners should always have a pre-prepared piece of work ('Here's one I made earlier!') to compare with their own, as this can result in learners over-emulating the sample work and not using their own skills of deduction to approach the task in an individual way. To curb this problem, try to provide several examples to illustrate alternative approaches. A worked copy of a similar, not identical, task can also be a good way to point them in the right direction without the temptation of copying.

Alternatively, try some of these strategies to bring modelling into the fabric of your learning environment and your lessons.

---

[1] See Edward de Bono, *Six Thinking Hats: An Essential Approach to Business Management* (Boston, MA: Little, Brown, & Company, 1985).

Strategy: WAGOLL (Boasting Board)

WAGOLL (What a Good One Looks Like) is very popular, especially in primary settings, and is often used in the classroom to create a fluid display of aspirational work. Displaying annotated work (it's often useful if the piece of work is enlarged for ease of reference) is an excellent way to celebrate best practice while highlighting the specific features that have made it successful.

A Boasting Board serves the same purpose: providing a place in the classroom to visibly share successful work with explicit reference to the aspects of the work that should be emulated. This is a brilliant way to foster a productive 'magpie' culture in the classroom (see Chapter 4), helping learners to see that the best examples are not exclusively those that come from the teacher and that their classmates can provide excellent resources too.

Using exemplar work is a great way to cut to the chase in your instructions about how to be successful in a piece of work: allow the learners to spot the best practice. This is often much clearer than explaining it verbally and provides an opportunity to engage with what the best practice looks like.

Strategy: Bad Teacher

In presenting the success steps to learners, the question 'What makes a great …?' is an excellent one to pose to the class. At times, however, we may be forgetting an uncomfortable truth about our learners: they are novices. Inherently, novices do not always have the in-built awareness and understanding to dutifully parrot back exactly what the key ingredients are to carrying out a task effectively. Surely, if the understanding was so firmly embedded that they are capable of articulating this without missing a beat, the challenge isn't sufficient. There should always be *some* element of discovery! There is also the question of confidence. A novice who is acquiring a skill may have a good idea about what success looks like, but may lack the confidence to share their impressions with their peers, as getting it wrong could feel embarrassing. Enter Bad Teacher.

While presenting themselves as an expert who can identify or describe best practice may feel uncomfortable, most learners are more than happy to don a pessimistic cap and spot the mistakes in something! Rather than showing your class examples of excellent practice to tease out the steps to success, show them an example that *lacks* all the key qualities of success and ask them to work together to decide what doesn't seem very good about the sample you've provided. The features that they identify as poor practice can be flipped into the positive elements that they need to include to excel in their own piece of work.

Creating a bad example can also be a worthwhile activity from the teacher's perspective. It allows you to anticipate the mistakes that you know your learners have a propensity for and illustrate them to the class without making use of an individual learner's poor effort.

Try This …

- Make a film of yourself doing something really badly and ask learners to watch and spot your mistakes.

- Ask learners to make their own 'How not to do it' video and share them with the class.

- Model a terrible opening sentence on the whiteboard.

- Demonstrate a poor example of how to carry out an experiment.

Strategy: Progress Portfolios

Modelling doesn't only have to be about showing final copies and best examples (as we've seen in Bad Teacher above). An important message to make clear in any classroom is that the path to 'greatness' is a journey, not a destination. Creating and meeting targets that help learners on this journey should form the foundation of progress in any classroom. However, it can be difficult to track the wide range of targets learners work at over a number of days, weeks or months.

Collecting together pieces of work that meet major targets or summative assessments that represent key gains in knowledge, skills or understanding in a portfolio is a good way to demonstrate progress made over time, and can be a great future resource. The portfolio need not be a record of 'best copy' or final drafts – it is incredibly valuable to track the evolution of a summative piece of work and include everything from planning and drafting to the final copy. Although some of the items in the file may not be pretty, it will illustrate the journey a learner has made in building skills, and reviewing and revising a piece of work. It will also make explicit to the learner, and any other stakeholder who views the portfolio, the hard work that has gone into the progress made.

Include lots of evidence in the portfolios, such as photographs, photocopies of formative pieces from learners' exercise books, mind maps, marked (peer or teacher) drafts or self-assessed copies. By saving the work in all the states in which it has appeared, you are also reinforcing the idea that it is not just the final copy that counts. To acknowledge and to be able to reflect on the key steps to success along the way to the final copy is important. The progress portfolio models the process of arriving at a piece of work that represents your very best effort.

The collection of this evidence will be a collaborative effort between the teacher and the learners, and the level of pupil involvement and autonomy in this will depend greatly on the age group you are teaching. Learners of any age will need it made explicit to them what items should be included. If your learners are managing the assembly of their own portfolios, they will need specific training in how you want it presented.

'What makes a great …?' is a question that should always be at the heart of our lessons, both as a question we ask ourselves as part of the planning process and one that we ask our learners to consider as well. Make this clear, couple it inextricably with your learning objectives and you should start buying gold stars in bulk – because you will be putting a lot of them on your marking!

Chapter 4

Making Collaborative Work Work!

Learner-Led Lessons with Real Impact

Ever had a genuine desire to use group work in your lesson (you know that your learners *could* gain a great deal from it) but there's a niggling worry that makes you hesitate? That niggling worry that you may be about to hand over your authority, your reputation and your sanity to a bunch of overenthusiastic but aimless individuals? The key thing that tends to worry us when it comes to letting learners work in groups is the fact that, all of a sudden, learner activity and participation can become invisible. Who knows if Sean is taking over in his group at the expense of his less confident teammates? Who knows if Chelsea is opting out altogether, or if Rhianna has been counselled into the passive role of scribe *again*? And since it can sometimes feel like everything rides on whether you can entrust hard work and responsibility to a bunch of youngsters who, quite frankly, you might not trust with your spare biro, can you be certain that the next 15 minutes are not going to be a waste of valuable time?

As teachers, we need to feel confident that small group work and paired work will *work*. You're bound to hear the odd colleague who will insist that group work impedes progress or is generally inferior to independent work, but these are usually the colleagues who have not yet discovered the ways to make group work effective, purposeful and progress focused. Using collaborative work in lessons can enhance learning in many ways:

- Discussing something helps us to retain it in the memory.

- It provides opportunities for learners to develop communication skills and learn how ideas are best articulated.

- It provides opportunities for learners to develop interpersonal and negotiating skills.

- It can encourage different social and cultural groups to interact and work together.

- It fosters a classroom expectation that learners will be active, responsive participants.

- It can teach the important workplace skill of working as part of a team, while still retaining a strong sense of individual accountability.

- It helps learners to understand that responsibility for personal success lies in their own hands.

- Ideas can be developed and clarified through discussion.

- Understanding is enhanced and elevated in our own minds when we teach that concept to someone else.

- It allows the teacher to circulate, observe and instantaneously assess, intervene and gather feedback.

- Problem-solving can be modelled by one learner for another.

- It allows for more innovative, engaging teaching techniques.

- Team competition can be a great intrinsic motivator.

- Once they have gained confidence from discovering that teammates share their confusion, learners are more likely to ask the teacher the questions they need answering in order to close the gaps in their knowledge.

- Learners can feel that they are more 'a part of' the lesson.

- English as an Additional Language (EAL) learners benefit enormously from interactions which involve using language through talk.

- The understanding of less able learners can be greatly enhanced by working closely with their more able peers.

■ It helps learners to stop seeing the teacher as the *only* source of knowledge.

If you need any more persuading about the value of group work, then think back again to those staff development days. If the presentation is engaging and thought-provoking, we audience members crave the moment when we're told that we've got some discussion time – the opportunity to actually get on and apply the magic together, to share all the ideas we've had buzzing around our head, to find out what the person next to us has made of the information and how they intend to use it.

So, how do we stop group work becoming the dreaded 'G' word? In this chapter, you'll find lots of techniques that can be used to scaffold and rein in group discussion tasks, so that you can feel secure in the knowledge that your learners are benefitting appropriately from collaborating.

Fluid Seating Plan

If allowed, youngsters will select their 'best friend forever' and ceremoniously sit next to them, and only them, in every single lesson and for every single task. While this is quite understandable (and we teachers may well do the same in the staffroom!), it's not always helpful for learners to work with the same person(s) day in, day out. As a skilful teacher who has an intricate knowledge of their learners' strengths and weaknesses, an important part of differentiation in the classroom is being able to consider what groupings would work well for a particular activity. Jennifer may benefit from working with Donna for a task that requires quickly generating ideas, but she may gain more from working with Oscar on a task that requires problem-solving skills.

Once you have established your classroom as a safe and positive environment, you should be able to maintain a fairly fluid seating plan. Create the expectation that learners will discover who they will be sitting and working with today on entering your room. You might find it useful to group names together on lolly sticks on a table for learners to consult as they walk in, or project a seating plan onto the board or place name-cards on the chairs. The greater the variety of peers that they have a chance to work with, the less likely it is for complacent behaviour patterns to set in among friendship groups during collaborative work.

Purposeful Talk

As mentioned in Chapter 2, just because you put learners in a small-group situation and give them a topic, problem or question to discuss, it does not mean that they suddenly turn into articulate, acutely focused debaters who would put a late-night BBC2 discussion panel to shame. A mistaken assumption that young learners are automatically equipped with the kind of interpersonal skills necessary to take part in meaningful, explorative discussion is what often causes group work to result in – well, poop work! Learners need to be helped to interact in a purposeful, useful way during group discussion. A simple buzzing timer on each table, for example, can be a great way to increase the level of focus and encourage a sense of urgency about the task. The String Thing technique (see Chapter 3) is an effective way to get learners to become aware of their 'discussion behaviour' and encourage them to analyse the format and nature of their dialogue.

Strategy: The Conch

A plainer version of the String Thing (for classes full of little munchkins who are likely to accidentally get themselves wrapped up like brown paper parcels) is, of course, the Conch concept. (If you haven't read *Lord of The Flies*, where a bunch of children turn into feral savages, you've probably witnessed something similar at Friday afternoon home time.) The conch was a shell used by the children in Golding's *Lord of the Flies* to bring order to their group discussions: to speak, you had to be holding the conch shell. With young children, having a special object like this that gets passed around can be an easy way to reinforce the importance of listening to one person at a time and then responding appropriately.

Another very effective strategy for enhancing the efficiency of small group work is to use Talk Tokens.

Strategy: Talk Tokens

When learners are required to discuss something in small groups, give each of them several tokens (six is a good amount for a 5–10 minute discussion). Some of these tokens should be 'contribution tokens' and others should be 'question tokens'. It will be up to you to decide how many of each learners should have – it will likely depend on the task. Explain the Talk Tokens rules carefully:

1   You will have a specified amount of time in which to have your discussion.

2   Each time you want to make a contribution to your group's discussion, you must 'spend' one of your contribution tokens (by placing it in the middle of the table).

3   Each time you want to ask a question of someone (or everyone) as part of the discussion, you must 'spend' one of your question tokens.

4   If you are speaking you must be spending.

5   You must spend all your tokens before the time is up.

6   Once your tokens are spent, you will need to concentrate on listening only.

The first time you try this strategy, some learners will find it extremely frustrating to have their contributions managed so tightly. However, persevere, because once you help learners to become adept in the art of talking with tokens, a number of breakthroughs occur:

■ The learner who would naturally monopolise discussion to the detriment of others, or engage in inapt waffle, suddenly finds that they have a finite number of contributions they can make. They abruptly realise that they need to make those limited inputs count. Consequently, they end up listening more carefully and composing their contributions more carefully in order to build on the ideas of others and add value to the discussion.

■ Sometimes a group has a passenger in their midst whose non-participation would normally be unnoticed by the other participants. With the requirement for tokens to be spent, the group becomes aware of this passivity and the passenger is encouraged by their peers to get involved.

■ Learners soon realise that the question tokens can be used to help another teammate to enter the discussion.

■ The question tokens serve to emphasise the importance of asking questions in the classroom, so learners dare to share the gaps in their understanding as well as probe topics to further their understanding (see Chapter 5 for more ideas on this).

■ The very able learner who might normally contribute five brilliant points to a group discussion, and then feel thoroughly satisfied with their offerings, suddenly finds her/himself holding a sixth token. Consequently, they are challenged to come up with an additional idea or question to move the discussion forward – a contribution which they would otherwise never have stretched themselves to think of.

Once you know your class really well, you should be able to differentiate for learners with varying needs by allocating different numbers of tokens to different learners:

'Jessica, today I'm going to give you one more question token than the other people in your group, because I know you'll make even faster progress if you ask more questions.'

'Gautam, I'm going to give you one more contribution token than the others because I really want you to start expressing all those excellent ideas you have in your head.'

'Harry, I'm going to give you one less contribution token today because I want you to work on your target of making sure that your contributions are always relevant, useful and carefully thought-out.'

This kind of personalisation of the learning experience, if handled sensitively, can encourage learners to focus precisely on the skills they need to develop in collaborative work and make them gleefully aware of how much you know and care about their individual needs.

Strategy: The Silent Discussion

An alternative way to get a handle on learners' contributions in a group discussion is to, on the odd occasion, instruct them that they may only communicate with each other through the medium of writing. Tell participants that there must be absolute silence in the room. If you are asking them to discuss a controversial topic, and someone wishes to express indignation, they must use a graphological device such as capital letters, underlining or exclamation marks to convey this tone. If someone is amused by what their teammate 'says' on paper, they must 'laugh on paper' (LOL!) or perhaps even use a relevant emoticon.

By taking away all paralinguistic and prosodic devices, such as tone, volume, pitch and gesture, you are making learners focus intently on the lexical articulation of their ideas. This, of course, means that learners become aware of the need to raise the quality of their writing in order for their contributions to be received as they would wish. A silent discussion like this also gives a voice to learners who get anxious about speaking up in front of others. In fact, if you allow learners to debate, on paper, a topic about which they have strong feelings, it is likely you will see learners feeling liberated to contest and dispute in ways which they would not normally feel able.

For learners who are not confident writers and find the practice of expressing themselves in sentences and paragraphs difficult, this can be an excellent developmental activity. By liberating learners from the need to follow strict rules of grammar and punctuation, and allowing them to communicate through their written stream of consciousness, they can focus on their ideas rather than technical accuracy.

Try This ...

Give each individual in the group a different coloured felt-tip pen. As the Silent Discussion unfolds, you will soon be able to see whether all members of the group are contributing equally. In fact, you will find that you suddenly have access to every learner's every contribution!

Moreover, with this colour-identification strategy, each learner becomes very aware of how much they are contributing to their group's discussion, as well as what they are 'hearing' from others.

Allocating Group Roles

Ever been at a staff meeting where too many people want to take the role of the 'problem spotter' ('That won't work because …', 'The problem with that is …')? Or where, all at once, too many colleagues want to take charge of the discussion ('I don't think we should waste any more time on this', 'Can we go back to the last point, please?')? Even worse, have you ever sat in a meeting where lots of talking takes place but nothing really gets achieved and no subsequent action is planned? Our guess is that, like us, you probably have …

If even socially skilled adults can end up in unproductive patterns of behaviour during formal discussions, then it's hardly surprising that young children or teenagers can too. Defining and allocating clear roles to participants is an effective way to scaffold small-group discussion and ensure that learners remain determined and purposeful.

The types of roles that you decide to allocate are entirely up to you, and will depend on both the nature of the task at hand and on your intricate knowledge of the individual participants. The important thing here is that you are the omniscient power that dishes out the roles – you know which learners you wish to challenge with which 'job description' and why you want to encourage them to exercise those particular skills. Left to make their own choice about their role, learners are likely to fall straight into their well-used comfort zones. By carefully allocating certain roles to certain learners, we can stretch and challenge them to develop new skills, come up with ideas they wouldn't normally have had and experience a real sense of achievement by trying something new and perhaps a little bit scary.

You will probably want to invent your own roles which are most relevant to the group task you are setting. However, there are some which will enhance most group work, so you might also wish to take your pick from the selection below:

Role	Job Description
Task Master	■ Contributes thoughtful and relevant ideas ■ Moderates discussion to ensure everyone stays on task ■ Ensures that other group members are fulfilling their roles ■ Ensures that everyone is contributing and encouraging people who seem to be holding back ■ Ensures that everyone's opinions are being heard and respected (no one dominates, interrupts, makes fun, etc.)
Time Lord	■ Contributes thoughtful and relevant ideas ■ Knows how much time they have for the task and budgets it accordingly (How much time should they spend discussing? Producing the work? Checking the work over? Summarising ideas?) ■ Makes sure the group does not spend too much time on one thing ■ Reminds the group how much time they have spent and how much they have left at appropriate intervals

Role	Job Description
Information Guru	■ Contributes thoughtful and relevant ideas ■ Records the information and ideas shared ■ Organises information into legible and well-presented notes or some other relevant form ■ Collates the ideas shared by all group members
Consolidation Clerk	■ Contributes thoughtful and relevant ideas ■ Checks that all group members understand the task they have been set ■ Asks group members to clarify contributions that might not make sense to others ■ Works with the Information Guru and the Public Speaker to ensure that the final product is in the form required and is easily understood
Public Speaker	■ Contributes thoughtful and relevant ideas ■ Shares their group's findings with the rest of the class, summarising and consolidating where appropriate
Problem Spotter	■ Contributes thoughtful and relevant ideas ■ Considers the weaknesses or uncertainties in any argument put forward ■ Ensures that their teammates are not just accepting contributions without questioning them ■ Scrutinises any work produced for mistakes or for aspects that could be improved

Role	Job Description
Jack-Out-the-Box	■ Contributes thoughtful and relevant ideas ■ Considers an alternative for each idea put forward by a group member ■ Encourages their teammates to 'think outside the box' and not to be satisfied with their first, most obvious idea
Solution Finder	■ Contributes thoughtful and relevant ideas ■ For every problem that is identified by the Problem Spotter or another member of the group, they must find a workable solution ■ Helps their group focus to find solutions for the difficulties that arise
Evidence Chaser	■ Contributes thoughtful and relevant ideas ■ Finds the evidence for ideas shared, verifies the validity of claims and checks references carefully ■ Researches the information and data that their group need to complete the task

As you read through the table of descriptors, you probably had certain members of your class in mind. However, do remember to stretch learners' potential by coaxing them into a role that might initially be a little alien to them.

It's easy to see how many of these roles can be adapted for all age groups. You might want to provide badges for younger children to reinforce the sense of responsibility that accompanies the adoption of a new role. Relevant props can also play their part in raising awareness of the roles – for example, a timer for the Time Lord or a toy microphone for the Public Speaker. For an extra sense of intrigue, try placing coloured stickers on chairs as an indication of who you would like to undertake which role.

The Magpie

We don't normally endorse plagiarism and general theft of intellectual property in the classroom, but here's a great way to add an extra element of intrigue to group work, as well as to maximise learning and promote the sharing of expertise.

Strategy: Scouting for Pearls (of Wisdom)

Split group work into short, timed sections. At the end of each carefully timed episode shout 'Scout!' or 'Magpie!' (or perhaps use some other auditory cue, like a bell or klaxon). At these planned interludes, each group sends an elected member to move quickly around the room, peering at the work of other groups with a view to pinching great ideas and bringing them back to their own group for consideration. This 'magpie-ing' of ideas happens quickly and with a great sense of urgency each time. You'll find that groups get very excited and competitive about the ideas that their scouts manage to acquire, but they tend to be equally intrigued and pleased to see which of their ideas are admired and subsequently stolen by scouts from other groups.

A common side-effect of this strategy is that through the anticipation of stealing concepts from other groups, your learners experience a sense of accountability in terms of ensuring that their own group pulls its weight in this mass exchange of ideas. After all, there is a certain pride to be taken in having the ability to produce ideas that are good enough for someone to want to steal!

Of course, to encourage equal participation from all, and to make sure that everyone has a chance to stretch their legs, it's best to insist that all group members have a turn at Scouting for Pearls (of Wisdom).

We've Cracked It!

We've discussed the reasons why a teacher might harbour anxieties about using group work, but what about the reservations that the learners themselves might have? The scariest thing about collaborative work is that it usually involves solving a problem – therefore, if learners are going to do it properly, they have to experience being stuck. For authentic learning to take place – not just a parroting back or writing down of information that is not fully understood – a learner may well need to feel so confused that their brain hurts! Once you've got metaphorical steam coming out of their ears, there is a greater chance of a group experiencing that wonderful, exhilarating moment of realising that they've worked something out for themselves! They've cracked it! Together they've found a solution, and it feels amazing.

> It's worth remembering that if we don't get learners solving problems and creating hypotheses for themselves, if we continually teach by imparting information, explanations and solutions directly into their ears, then we deprive them of that unrivalled 'We've cracked it!' feeling.

Here is a collection of small group and pair activities, adaptable for any subject, that get the learners doing the work and that give them back that 'Cracked it!' moment.

Strategy: Life Is Like a Box of Chocolates

This strategy is a fantastic way to embrace the use of metaphors in making learning memorable and challenging learners to think about concepts they have learnt in a different context. The preparation is simple: gather together a collection of objects with interesting properties. Examples might include costume jewellery, small toys, key rings with obnoxious attachments, unusual kitchen utensils, gadgets ... the possibilities are endless. When in doubt, just go to that dodgy drawer that we *all* have in our kitchens (you know the one – it's where instruction manuals for appliances that you don't even own any more are kept) and go wild!

Arrange learners in small groups or pairs and provide each grouping with one of your random objects. Give learners 60 or 90 seconds to describe as many properties of the

object as possible using simple statements. For example, if your group had a pair of scissors, they would generate statements such as:

- They are sharp.

- They are hinged.

- They are shiny.

- They are smooth.

- They are potentially dangerous.

Once the learners have complied their lists, reveal to them the topic that you want them to make the connections with. Learners will then be challenged to make as many of their statements 'fit' the topic as possible. For example, if they were asked, 'How is your object like the Second World War?', the learners in the group with the scissors might say: 'The Second World War can be seen as "sharp" because attacks such as Dunkirk were sharply planned and executed. It could be seen as "hinged" because all the parts of the war effort (like producing supplies for the front lines, planning attacks and training soldiers) had to work together like a hinge to make things move. "Shiny" could represent propaganda because propaganda was used to glamorise the war and make it seem appealing. "Potentially dangerous" is a clear fit because many of the citizens of Europe were in a potentially dangerous situation.' And so on.

Not all of the connections made will be obvious ones – the more tenuous the link they are forced to make the better! Learners are forced to think intricately about qualities and underlying issues within the concept you have provided in order to make as many connections as possible. Some responses will be insightful, some will be silly. Both are valuable as they are asking for learners to connect with their learning and understanding in a different medium, thereby making the learning memorable. Add an element of competition by challenging the groups to make the largest number of responses, or perhaps by rewarding the most interesting link made.

Try This ...

Use Life Is Like a Box of Chocolates as an irresistible extension task for those bright sparks who finish early or whom you just want to stretch a little bit further. Simply hand them a random object and ask them to come up with as many examples as they can of why this item is akin to what they have just learnt about. This appealing, quirky task will force them to 'think around' the topic they have just covered in a probing way, and will require them to dredge up and consider everything they have learnt in order to forge connections.

Strategy: Strike a Pose[1]

When we want to get feedback from learners about their understanding, we can sometimes be a bit unimaginative about the format in which we request it. More often than not, we will ask learners to demonstrate what they know through answering our questions or through writing. However, it's useful to remember that while these might be our default methods, there are other ways to get crucial feedback from our learners about what they understand and where they're not quite hitting the mark. Strike a Pose is a fun and engaging way to get immediate visible feedback about learners' understanding and leaves no room for learners to hide their responses or lack of understanding.

As soon as you are ready to ascertain what new learning has occurred in your lesson, ask learners to work in small groups and get up out of their seats to discuss and compose a tableau (a still image) using their bodies to represent the knowledge they have just acquired from their reading or listening. This is best preceded by a carefully phrased question. Imagine, for example, the frozen scene a group of learners might discuss and strike up in response to questions like, 'What are the benefits of capitalism?', 'What does this source suggest were the instigators of Marilyn Monroe's death?', 'In what kind of real-life scenario would multiplication skills be useful?', 'What was the saddest part of the story?', 'How does the water cycle work?', 'How might an "arms race" be represented?' or 'How can you represent "imperialism"?'

---

[1] Creating tableaux to represent concepts is a long-established teaching technique, although it has been pioneered recently by Phil Beadle, in *How to Teach: The Book of Plenary* (Carmarthen: Independent Thinking Press, 2013), and others.

When groups strike their pose, other learners in the class can be encouraged to interpret the tableau or ask questions which the 'posers' must answer. In the case of a tableau about imperialism, for example, what might one hand high in the air and one hand low to the ground represent? Can learners contribute ideas about what those arms flexed in a 'muscle man' pose might signify about imperialism? How might perceptions of imperialism change if the learner has a smile on their face versus a furrowed brow? If learners work in pairs, what does a partner who is cowering in front of the 'muscle man' imply about imperialism? And so on.

The strategy allows for learners to respond in two ways: first, learners need to consolidate their understanding by choosing a way to physically represent key ideas they have encountered and, second, a discussion prompt is provided as they interpret their peers' poses.

Of course, to make learning even more memorable, digital photographs of the frozen pictures can be saved to comment on and/or annotate at a later date.

Strategy: Rounders

This activity works well in a competitive context. Split your class into teams (if you have 30 learners then this might be six groups of five). Give each team a large piece of flipchart or sugar paper (or a paper tablecloth, banquet roll or wallpaper) and try to ensure that each learner has a different coloured felt-tip pen. On your signal, teams must race to add as much information to the sheet as they can about the topic in hand, querying and building on each other's ideas. As you circulate around the classroom and observe the contributions, this activity will provide you with vital information about what the teams do or do not know.

On your second signal, learners must stop, leave their sheet of paper in place and move around to the next table where another group's collection of ideas will obviously be waiting for them. Once they have taken a few moments to read what the other group has written, learners should start adding to, responding to or improving the ideas or information on this sheet. On your third signal, groups must move around again and add to the next sheet. And so on. Eventually, the groups will arrive back at their original table and be able to scrutinise all the ideas, comments and embellishments that have been added to the ideas they had originally compiled as a group.

The benefits here are numerous. First, learners make considerable gains by pooling their ideas and having an opportunity to add to and improve their initial stab at the task. Second, learners get to be up and moving about – a great way to break the monotony of five hours' worth of sitting. But the thing that is especially magical about this little gem of strategy is that, if every learner has their own coloured pen, you can track their contributions around the classroom. If the additions in hot pink demonstrate impressive insight, then you will know that Amelia has attained a particularly high level of understanding and is perhaps ready to be stretched further. If the additions in light green demonstrate a number of misconceptions, then you will know that Matthew will require some tactful intervention. As a proficient chameleon teacher, you'll be in your element!

Try This ...

Here are a number of different ways in which Rounders can be used:

- A different question on each table.

- Redrafting and improving a piece of writing.

- Improving a picture.

- Adding to a model.

- Adding to and improving a sentence.

- Spotting features in a text or picture and highlighting them.

- Brainstorming ideas under different headings.

- Adding words that contain a certain suffix on each table.

- Synonyms for a different word on each table.

- A different answer on each table – learners provide the question.

Strategy: Sort It Out

Find out what learners already know or understand by asking them to complete a sorting activity in pairs or groups. This might involve matching questions with answers, matching extracts of work with success criteria or simply arranging different concepts or key words into relevant categories or hierarchical orders. Make sure learners are aware that the entire group is responsible for double-checking placement and that any one of them could be called on to explain their group's reasoning behind a particular arrangement of the components. As you circulate, it should become evident quite quickly which areas of the topic learners are unsure of or have misconceptions about. Use this information to ensure that your subsequent lesson addresses these identified needs.

Try This ...

You can spice up sorting activities by asking learners to use clothes pegs and a washing line to peg certain concepts together or in a particular meaningful order. Ideas can also be sequenced by using compartmental party plates, layered cake stands or by using simple containers or stackable objects such as paper cups.

Strategy: Crocodile Creek

This strategy works especially well when learners are organised into pairs. Each pair must create a grid, like the one below, to represent a crocodile-infested river.

The number of rows and columns that make up the creek will be entirely dependent on the topic and learning objective. The aim of the activity is to move a counter (an eraser or pencil sharpener will suffice) safely across the river, from the near-side to the far-side, by selecting one square from each of the rows. Each chosen square must link with the previous one in order to make a successful passage across.

For example, in order to cross the creek below from near-side to far-side, it would be necessary to compose a coherent three-word sentence by selecting one word from each row, followed by the appropriate punctuation. Successful routes across the creek would include 'I → love → sheep → !' or 'Who → likes → food → ?'

			.	!	?	.				
sleeps	sheep	you	he	there	eats	it	big	that	food	that
went	was	want	are	is	likes	cat	love	dad	over	just
Where	You	Is	I	My	There	He	The	Sit	How	Who

An example for numeracy might look like the grid below (with successful routes across the creek including calculations such as: '2 → x → 5 = 10' or '3 → ÷ → 3 = 1'.

28	12	10	15	6	9	8	24	1	5	0
	14	7	3	2	8	2	5	9	1	
		+	-	x	÷					
	2	8	5	3	4	10	1			

An example to help learners to explore key terms might look something like this:

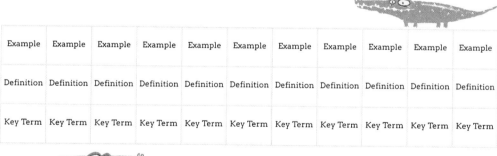

Example	Example	Example	Example	Example	Example	Example	Example	Example	Example	Example
Definition	Definition	Definition	Definition	Definition	Definition	Definition	Definition	Definition	Definition	Definition
Key Term	Key Term	Key Term	Key Term	Key Term	Key Term	Key Term	Key Term	Key Term	Key Term	Key Term

Once you begin to think about it the possibilities are endless. You can ask learners to create grids to connect:

- Historical event → key date → relevant person/s
- Past tense → present tense → future tense
- Synonyms
- Cause → effect → image
- Point → evidence → explanation

- Character → quote → significance

- Order in which to take steps in a process

- Sequencing of images in a narrative

- Letters to build words

- 2D shape name → 2D shape image → number of sides → number of vertices

- Chemical → chemical → reaction

- Life cycles

- Animal → habitat → food

- Fraction → decimal → percentage

Of course, making this sort of resource will require a great deal of careful thinking by the learners. They will need to review everything they have learnt so far about the topic in order to create a viable creek for other classmates to cross. Once pairs have created their Crocodile Creek, they should swap it with that of another pair and each team should keep a list of how many ways they find to successfully and accurately cross the river. After completing the task, they should share their routes with the originators of the creek and, if necessary, justify or question each other's decisions. If desirable, some squares might be left blank in order to force the learners to offer their own missing link in their chosen route across the river.

The beauty of this activity is that it encourages learners to make links and explore connections between the things they have been learning about. As their knowledge and understanding increase over the course of a scheme of work, learners can add further rows to their creeks, bringing in their newfound comprehension and thus seeing their river widen as their brains metaphorically expand.

Try This ...

To really bring the Crocodile Creek to life, organise learners into small groups and set the grids out on the floor (one piece of A4 paper per square) or take the class outside and chalk it onto the playground. As each learner literally makes their journey across the imaginary river, other members of the group can be encouraged to act as crocodiles – i.e. keep their eyes peeled for any mistakes the 'explorer' might make and ask them to justify their route if they deem it necessary.

Strategy: Scratch

While the name of this strategy may conjure up images of rashes or head lice (and if it didn't before, it does now!) what Scratch is actually about is getting learners to move beyond the obvious first solution/response and stretch to more creative, off-piste thinking.

First of all, devise a list of six to eight features or prompts about the topic you are studying or revising. It should be possible to provide several examples of each of the concepts you select. Consider the following prompts to support analysis of Act 1, Scene 2 of *Hamlet*:

- A quotation that shows Hamlet is depressed.

- An adjective that describes Hamlet's relationship with his mother.

- A metaphor illustrating a dark mood.

- An image of mourning.

- A pun.

- A classical allusion.

Or this selection of prompts for the topic of tourism:

- A country that relies on tourism as its main source of income.

- Something that is necessary in order for tourism to continue.

- A benefit of tourism.

- A reason why people might decide to tour other countries.

- An important development that might increase tourism.

- A popular tourist resort in the UK.

Or this selection of prompts for the topic of shapes:

- A 2D shape with more than four sides.

- A 2D shape with less than six vertices.

- An object which is cylindrical.

- A 2D shape with more than three lines of symmetry.

- A type of triangle.

- A shape you can see in this classroom.

Learners, in pairs or small groups, are then given two minutes to decide upon one possible response to each category with the understanding that they will only get points for a response that no other group has thought of. To debrief the responses, each group gets an opportunity to read out their choices; if no one else has thought of their particular response, they will be greeted with silence. If another group has also written down that response they shout 'Scratch!' (as in 'cross it out', not as in 'soothe an itch'!). This creates a great competitive vibe in the classroom and your learners will quickly embrace discussion and debate as they scramble for points and justify their choices. From a behaviour management perspective, you will need to lay down clear guidelines for how the students should challenge responses and engage in debate, as without careful handling it can turn into a shouting match. For example, Talk Tokens or The Conch (see Chapter 4) work brilliantly to ensure that only one learner speaks at a time and that they are listening to each other's responses.

Insisting that the groups choose only one response is beneficial from a discussion perspective because they are then forced to consider a unique response. They will avoid the most obvious idea – or the first one that occurs to them – as they know that another group may also respond with this. As an alternative, however, you can allow learners to include as many responses to each category as they have time for. This lengthens the debriefing process but allows learners to share a greater volume of suggestions.

Scratch lends itself well to close-text analysis and can give learners a strong focus in looking for information or text-level features. The choices they make for each category can also be used as the skeleton for a subsequent paragraph or essay response.

Strategy: The Line-Up

You've seen the scene in a movie where a police officer parades a little old lady along a line of potential culprits to identify the perpetrator of the crime. Well, this activity will have your classroom resembling that scenario somewhat (with you as the little old lady – sorry, tough, young teacher-blokes!).

Divide your class into groups of about seven or eight learners. Give each group a set of seven or eight words, images, numbers, statements or characters on paper so that each learner has one piece of paper to hold. Get the learners up on their feet and ask them to stand in a row (e.g. if you have a class of 30, you will have four groups and therefore a line of learners standing along each of the four walls of your classroom).

Once the learners are in position, you can ask them to arrange themselves into a particular order – for example, if each of them is holding part of the Cinderella story (in text or picture form) you might ask them to organise themselves according to the sequential order of the story. If they are each holding a statement about sex before marriage, you might ask them to arrange themselves according to which sentiment they most agree with from least popular to most popular. If they are holding past kings and queens, you might ask them to stand in order of reign. If they are holding descriptions of the steps involved in a scientific experiment, you might ask them to organise themselves into the correct order in which the steps should be completed – or in order of which step is most crucial, or even (for a nice bit of personal response) which step they most enjoy carrying out. In fact, once you've got the kids standing in rows, there are likely to be many different ways in which to challenge, probe and extend their thinking.

For example, imagine what you would do if each learner was holding a character from *Macbeth*:

'OK everyone, when I say "Go!" each group must organise themselves into a line that shows which character died from first to last ...'

'Now, arrange yourselves according to whom you feel was most responsible for all those deaths – from least responsible to most responsible.'

'Alright, now you've got to order yourselves into a line that indicates which character you would least like to have dinner with – from least desirable to most desirable.'

And so on.

Of course, some of the instructions will lead to far more debate than others. If you're asking the learners to organise themselves chronologically, for example, then there is likely to be a clear right or wrong order. If, on the other hand, your instruction requires personal opinion then the task may require a significant amount of deliberation and you may need to give a time limit to support them in reaching a conclusion sometime this decade!

When the groups have organised themselves into their lines, it is time to encourage them to compare their order with that of the other groups. At this point, you get to be that little old lady because you can walk up and down the lines, asking learners to justify their own and their teammates' positions.

The pure physicality of this activity can allow even abstract concepts to suddenly become clear. Rendering physical – tangible even – the sequencing or hierarchy of ideas can be a powerful demystifier when it comes to complex thinking and embedding learning into the memory. Furthermore, this type of 'take a stand' activity can inspire potentially apathetic or indifferent youngsters to actually have an opinion on an important topic and learn how to justify their views.

Try This ...

The Line-Up could be used to explore any of the following:

- The order in which tasks should be performed.
- The order of 'most likely'.
- The order of importance.
- Chronological order.
- Sequencing.

- Synonyms – strongest to weakest.

- Structuring ideas in an essay.

- Order of steps to take to tackle a problem.

- Most likeable to least likeable – justify or explain.

- Letters in a word.

- Words in a sentence.

- Grading anonymous samples of work.

- Most relevant to least relevant.

This strategy, as with most, relies on you asking just the right questions to get them thinking in just the right ways, and on the learners asking themselves and each other questions that drive their learning forward.

If you're looking for more ways to build effective questioning (both teacher's and learners') into any lesson, simply turn to the next chapter where a whole host of practical strategies awaits you!

Chapter 5

It's Only Easy If You Know the Answer

Questioning Strategies That Support and Stretch

The questions that teachers ask in a lesson should be seen as the vehicles that drive the learning. It is better, then, to ensure that we have prepared to launch a fleet of powerful jumbo jets rather than a host of flimsy paper aeroplanes. If there is one part of a lesson that always needs careful consideration and planning, no matter how busy the teacher is, then it's the questions they are going to ask. The quality of your questions will govern the quality of learning and the progress that learners make.

Yet far too often we question in a way that is simply not conducive to deepening our learners' understanding. Many of us tend to have default questioning 'modes' which we use without thinking. Often, our automatic approach to questioning learners is driven by a desire to elicit the response we are thinking of as swiftly as we possibly can. (If you're feeling really brave, you might like to have yourself filmed while teaching to get an accurate picture of your most common questioning styles!)

In this chapter, you'll find a variety of ways to get your learners doing the lion's share of the thinking. You'll find techniques which will help you to ensure that your own questions are useful and well-targeted. We've also included a number of strategies for helping learners to develop, ask and answer their *own* questions.

Let's start by taking a look at one of the most common teacher questioning crimes: *rephrasing, in a more eloquent way, every answer your learners give.* Convinced that you're not guilty of this? Watch yourself *really* carefully. We tend to experience an instinctive urge to take a learner's oral contribution and restate it for the whole class in a more articulate and superior form. Hell, we'll pull this 'repeat or rephrase' trick even when our most articulate learner makes a perfectly clear and fluent contribution! Of course, occasionally it *is* necessary to rephrase something a learner has said for the benefit of the whole class, particularly if we're trying to reinforce correct pronunciation, vocabulary or sentence structure. But, if we condition learners to assume that we're going to repeat or rearticulate every one of their classmates' contributions, then two very dangerous things can happen. And they *do* happen – in thousands of classrooms every day.

First, learners learn not to listen to each other. 'Why bother?' they ask themselves. 'If Sir or Miss is shortly going to repeat this in a more articulate form, then why do I need to make the effort to engage with what my classmate is saying right now?' The everyday effect of this is that learners learn to automatically tune out when a classmate begins to talk and tune back in again when the teacher starts speaking. This is the reason why getting one learner to respond to another's assertions is often far harder than we feel it ought to be. It is the cause of that age-old scenario familiar to every teacher: 'What an excellent point, Lucy. James, did you hear what Lucy just said? No, you didn't, did you? Because you weren't listening, were you? ... Lucy, please could you just say that again?' And so on.

Try This ...

Have your learners filmed during a lesson. Observe carefully what happens when one learner answers one of your questions in a 'whole-class context'.

- Do you notice a difference in learners' attention levels between parts of the lesson when the teacher is addressing the class and the parts when a classmate is answering a question?

- Is there anything in the class's behaviour to suggest that when an individual begins to offer an answer to a teacher's question, this exchange is interpreted as a private conversation and not of relevance to the rest of the class?

- What can you glean about whether learners are, or are not, listening to classmates' responses to your questions?

> How many times do you rearticulate learners' oral contributions for them?

Second, when learners know that you are likely to repeat their answer, they allow themselves to be very lazy about the way they express their ideas. Why put the effort into articulating a carefully worded, powerful response to a question when you have your very own teacher-genie just waiting to take your mumbled monosyllabic grunt and magically transform it into something impressive sounding? Most teachers are no stranger to a version of the following conversation:

Teacher: Toby, why do you think Romeo refuses to fight Tybalt?

Toby: I dunno.

Teacher: Well, have a think about it.

Toby: (Thinks) … I dunno.

Teacher: I'm sure you do, if you just think a little harder … Why might Romeo want to avoid fighting with Tybalt, his new wife's cousin?

Toby: He doesn't feel like fighting?

Teacher: OK! Yes! Right! So he doesn't feel like fighting because he knows that fighting with anyone could get him executed – which would mean he wouldn't get to enjoy a life married to Juliet. And he particularly doesn't want to fight Tybalt because he's now related by marriage to him and it would be considered very wrong to attack your own family – not to mention how it would upset Juliet. So, as Toby says, Romeo really needs to avoid this fight if he can …

In this scenario, the teacher works far harder than the learner and any learning and progress is dubious and certainly not demonstrable. So, what can we do to reduce the number of times situations like this occur? After all, if we provide this premium editing service for learners all the time, then we set them up for failure in examinations where they suddenly realise that there is no magic service available to formulate their ideas into coherent sentences for them.

The solution? Keepy-Uppy Questioning!

Strategy: Keepy-Uppy Questioning

First of all, we need to train learners out of expecting their and their classmates' contributions to be automatically repackaged and presented to them again in 'teacher-speak'. Many learners have undergone years of this experience and their expectation that the teacher will repeat all contributions is no longer even a conscious one. We need to condition learners to be ready to listen to each other, to be alert the first time around and to be responsive to their classmates' ideas.

Keepy-Uppy Questioning is a great way to ensure that learners are on their toes and ready to listen and respond to one another during class discussion. You must commit to stepping away from the spotlight and abandoning the traditional pattern of: teacher asks question, learner answers, teacher clarifies. Instead you will embrace a new pattern – one where the focus is on the learners and the quality of their answers. Once learners begin to realise that their classmates are relying on clear, worthwhile contributions from *them*, the quality of their answers will naturally and necessarily improve. The approach takes genuine commitment and patience, but once it is embedded, questioning and discussion will henceforward sound something like this:

Teacher: Toby, why do you think Romeo refuses to fight Tybalt?

Toby: Because he doesn't feel like fighting?

Teacher: Mark, what can you add to Toby's response?

Mark: Romeo is scared of getting into a fight with Tybalt because Tybalt's well 'ard.

Teacher: Jemma, what do you think of that suggestion?

Jemma: I think Romeo doesn't want to fight Tybalt because he's supposed to love Tybalt now because he's just married a Capulet.

Teacher: Sally, would you change any of what Jemma just said?

Sally: I don't think he feels he ought to love Tybalt, I just think he doesn't want to upset Juliet by fighting with her cousin.

Teacher: Hayley, what did Sally just say?

Hayley: Erm … she said Romeo's more worried about how fighting with Tybalt would upset Juliet than anything else.

And so on.

In this scenario, the discussion is being metaphorically volleyed from one class member to the next, with an expectation that no one will 'drop the ball'. This is the essence of Keepy-Uppy Questioning.

The first time you try Keepy-Uppy Questioning with an uninitiated class, you may find it goes more like this:

Teacher: Toby, why do you think Romeo refuses to fight Tybalt?

Toby: Because he doesn't feel like fighting?

Teacher: Mark, what can you add to Toby's response?

Mark: Umm … Sorry? What? … I didn't hear what Toby said. What did ya say, Tobes?

And that is when the horrible realisation creeps over you: *most of the time, when one learner is answering your question, many class members automatically tune out.*

So if ever there was a top tip for using Keepy-Uppy Questioning in your lessons it is this: *tell your class you are going to be using the Keepy-Uppy technique.* Learners will soon come to realise that they have to be consistently attentive throughout whole-class discussion and question time because the question could be volleyed in *anyone's* direction at *any* moment. You can even challenge them to beat their class record by seeing how far they can explore and build on each other's ideas.

Try using questions like:

- What could you add to that?

- What would you challenge about that response?

- What evidence is there for that response?

- How do you think [name] reached that conclusion?

- How could we prove that right or wrong?

- What might an alternative interpretation look like?

- Would the same answer apply if …?

- What did [name] just say?

- What do you think of that response?

- Why might someone disagree with that response?

Try This ...

Once you have planned your Keepy-Uppy questions (and you *will* need to plan them in order to keep up the momentum once the exercise starts), use your excellent knowledge of individuals to target the right question at the right learner. This way you can stretch, challenge and support appropriately to differentiate for the varying needs of your class members.

Avoiding a Question Pile-Up

Another common questioning error in the classroom is the loading of question on top of question without giving learners enough time to answer them. We teachers have a tendency to do this when we're particularly anxious to get an answer and move on to all the other content we need to cover, or else when deep down we lack faith in our learners' ability to work something out on their own. In lessons, it usually goes something like this:

Teacher: Jordan, how do we change *je mange* to the past tense? Do you remember? The lesson we did yesterday?

(Jordan hesitates …)

Teacher: What did we have to do to the word *je*? And what do we have to do to the end of verbs to change them into the past tense?

(Jordan hesitates …)

Teacher: Can you remember what we do to the 'e' on the end of *mange*? Can you remember what we put on top of it?

This is a fairly typical example of a teacher trying to support her learners through questioning. But in this short time (about 45 seconds) *seven* questions are asked. And, having had his thinking process constantly interrupted since the original question was posed, Jordan is likely to still be thinking about the first question – or the second – or perhaps, now, the most recent one.

Learners need thinking time. Being bombarded with well-meaning, mind-jogging questions can often make their minds want to jog right off out of the classroom. What Jordan needs is the acknowledgement that needing a little time to consider the question and formulate an answer is perfectly acceptable (and reassuringly human!). What he needs is the 10-Second Rule.

Strategy: The 10-Second Rule

Imagine, for a moment, that you are a learner, sitting in a classroom full of your peers and the teacher poses the following question to you all: 'What is 14 x 15?'

What is your immediate reaction? Did you calculate the answer? For many of us, our brain quickly assesses the question to establish whether it will require significant thinking or working-out time. In a classroom scenario, we may well conclude immediately that there is no point trying to work that one out because 'someone else will answer or be called on to answer before I've found the answer myself'. We may even not attempt to formulate an answer simply because it requires effort that we don't feel like expending.

Imagine, now, that you know you will have 10 seconds to think about the answer before anyone is allowed to raise their hand. This is a powerful trick which encourages learners to kick-start their brains into gear and begin the process of finding a possible answer to a question. Most learners just need a little time to think before they can articulate a meaningful answer, and yet time to think is often a rare commodity in lesson time. Silence can feel very awkward during teacher Q&A sessions, but we should try to combat the false notion that someone must *always* be talking if learning is to be taking place.

So, try this in your classroom: tell your class that you're going to be using the 10-Second Rule for important questions this lesson. Explain to them that once you have posed a question, *no one* may raise their hand to answer the question for 10 seconds. *After* 10 seconds have passed, learners may raise their hand if they would like to suggest an answer to your question. Not only will you find that a far greater number of learners than usual raise their hands to suggest an answer, but the answers themselves are likely to be more articulate owing to the contemplation and preparation time.

Bear in mind that even if the 10 seconds do not result in learners answering 'correctly', you can pat yourself on the back, proud in the knowledge that you have engineered something quite amazing inside those little heads – you have driven them to activate the cerebral gear for thinking. Speaking of gears, remember too, that often when we pose a question to an entire class, many learners don't even have a chance to get the key into the ignition before someone is selected to answer!

If you need any more convincing about the power of the 10-Second Rule, try giving an immediate answer to the following questions:

■ What is your favourite song of all time?

■ What five things might an astronaut worry about?

■ If you could live your adolescence over again, what is the one thing you wouldn't do again?

■ What are the names of all Santa's reindeers?

This technique can also be coupled with the 'no-hands' rule to increase accountability for devising an answer. If, at the end of the thinking time, learners know that you will ask whoever you like for a response, rather than just those who raise their hands, further impetus is created for them to have *something* to say.

So, what do you do when, after providing thinking time and asking a learner of your choice for a response, they respond with 'Uh … I dunno'? One response that you should *not* provide is, 'Oh, OK,' and proceed to ask someone else. Instead, let the learner know that you are going to ask two or three of their peers for an answer and that, afterwards, they will need to summarise their peers' points. You could also ask them to offer some sort of extension to one of their peers' responses by using a Keepy-Uppy question stem.

Strategy: Rehearse and Report

Another very simple way that we can support learners in answering our questions more confidently and articulately is to allow them time to rehearse a possible answer with a partner. Instead of designating 10 seconds of silent thinking time, allocate a slightly longer period of time (depending on the nature of the question) for each learner to turn to another and briefly hash out a potential solution or response. Once the rehearsal time is up, a learner who is selected to give their response should feel more confident (because they've already shared their idea and had it validated by someone else) and is likely to be more articulate (because they've already expressed it verbally once). This strategy also helps to ensure that every learner actively engages with the question and gives it some consideration.

This is not a waste of time, but rather a valuable step in helping individuals to overcome their anxieties about contributing to discussions or asking an all-important question. Most of us will have had that experience when, sat in a meeting or presentation, we have suddenly wanted to ask for clarification or contribute a point. However, on this particular occasion, we didn't quite have enough confidence in the relevance of our question or the validity of our assertion to dare utter it in front of the whole group. So what did we do? We whispered that question or assertion to the person we were sitting next to. We tried it out on them first! We wanted to use their reaction to gauge whether this would be a reasonable statement to make or question to pose. Once they had validated our whispered words with their enthusiastic nodding, we felt brave enough to raise our query or put our point to the whole room. Had our neighbour frowned and shifted his seat away from us, we might have thought twice about sharing our idea publicly …

When you're a youngster, this painful fear of inadvertent self-humiliation can be amplified several times over. In fact, it's important to remember that for some learners, the very idea that they might be suddenly selected to answer a question can have them in a state of terror from the moment that a Q&A session begins.

Strategy: The Lesson Trailer

When you watch a good trailer for a good film, it gives you a little preview of the movie and it also gets you *wondering*, *conjecturing* and *speculating*. In fact, movie trailers often feature questions in the form of captions appearing on the screen or via the booming vocals of the voiceover man: 'Who will be next?' 'Is there anyone who can save them all before it's too late?' etc.

If your lesson is going to be driven by a number of extremely important questions, then consider displaying these questions from the moment your lesson begins. Having the key questions in mind from the outset can help learners to have a clearer sense of the lesson's purpose and can also give them that bit of extra time needed by some to mull over and formulate the kind of response that reflects their true ability.

If you have had your key questions on display from the moment your learners entered the classroom, they will be in a better position to answer those questions when you eventually reach the appropriate moment in the lesson. At some point in our lives, we've all heard someone say, 'I need to go away and think about that' or 'Can I get back to you on that?' Since this generally means that the person will be giving your question the attention it deserves, then it's usually a good sign (unless you've just made a marriage proposal – in that case, it's not a good sign at all!).

Celebrating Learners' Questions

Teacher questioning is always an avidly debated topic, but what about *learners'* questioning habits? It's a sad fact that many learners equate asking a question with being unintelligent. And yet we know that learners who ask questions do better at school. Questions are how we make progress, how we close gaps for ourselves and open new ones to cross. Fear and disparagement of questions is a classroom culture that we have to challenge. It's sometimes too easy to see learners' questions as irritants to the smooth flow of our lessons, when they should be viewed as a positive – great lessons should be making learners want to ask questions.

We could even argue that, in a great lesson, the learners should be encouraged to ask more questions than the teacher asks. After all, answering a question often only involves showing what you already know, whereas asking a question allows you to learn something new. What better evidence is there of learner engagement, of organic differentiation and individualised learning? What better way for the teacher to get feedback about the impact of their own teaching and about what the learners have understood and what they haven't, about what interests them and what doesn't, about when to move on and when to wait and consolidate?

When we see or hear something that captures our interest, it makes us want to know more. Just cast your mind back to the last social event you attended. When you splurged those 'interesting' anecdotes about yourself, the response you were hoping for from your captivated audience was 'Tell me more!'. You didn't want polite silence and an unnatural absence of questions. If our audience is alert and intrigued, then they will want to investigate further the information we are sharing. We should keep this is mind when we are teaching: if we have been successful in planning an engaging, interesting lesson, then our learners will naturally be wondering and questioning, so we should ensure that we have built into our lesson at least one way to draw out and celebrate these wondering questions. Here are a few tried-and-tested strategies to help you do just that.

Strategy: Passing Notes

Do you remember getting told off at school for passing notes in class? That age-old teenage tradition is now rapidly being replaced by its 21st century counterpart – under-the-desk messaging via their chosen mode of social media. Well, for old time's sake, let's resurrect that antiquated ritual of passing notes via a lovely lesson activity that really encourages active learning.

We have to encourage enquiring minds, so this activity does just that. It provides an opportunity for learners to think about the questions they might still have about a topic – the things that they are *wondering*.

Each learner must write down one question they would like answered about the topic on a piece of paper and then fold it over as if it's a secret note. As soon as they are ready, stick some music on. The learners all pass their notes clockwise around the class (it doesn't really matter if they get muddled) until you stop the music. When the music stops, each learner must open up whatever note they are holding.

At this point, there are several ways to run the activity. One of our favourites (if you have asked learners to pass around their questions at the beginning of the lesson) is to ask learners to keep the note they have received a secret. Their unique mission is then to see if they can find an answer to this question in the learning that occurs during the ensuing lesson. At the end of the lesson, learners can be invited to read out the question they ended up holding and, hopefully, offer a suggested answer or, alternatively, open it up for debate. If no one in the class can answer the question, then this is a valuable tool for informing your planning of subsequent lessons (or a handy little research question for homework!).

An alternative take on this strategy is to address the questions within the main body of your lesson. In this case, learners can consider the question they are holding and must then go and research the question and produce an answer. Answers can be submitted to you for perusal and returned to the author of the question later on. Alternatively, those carefully researched written answers could be displayed in an easily accessible place for all your learners to consult – perhaps on your Wonderwall (see below). A shorter version of this activity is achieved by asking learners to write down a question about the topic that requires a concise, factual answer. In this way, when the notes have been passed, learners can be called on to read out the questions they are holding and attempt to answer them then and there!

This activity is simple but effective: it involves every learner in the classroom (so there are no passengers), it encourages learners to ask questions, it facilitates independent research skills and it allows you to identify areas of the topic that still require clarification. Best of all, it's fun, it's intriguing and it's designed specifically to close gaps in the learners' knowledge.

Strategy: Wonderwall

Named by lovers of alliteration (or lovers of Oasis), a Wonderwall is one of the most valuable resources you can have as a permanent feature in any classroom. A Wonderwall is an area allocated for learners to post any questions that they have about the learning during the lesson. It is not intended to replace the traditional 'hands-up-and-ask' approach, but rather to offer an additional vehicle for individual learners or small groups to share what they are wondering about without interrupting the flow of the lesson. The Wonderwall sends a clear message to learners: 'In this classroom, your questions are not only welcome – they are desired. If you are working well and focusing on today's learning, then you *will* have questions. Please make a note of them and post them on the Wonderwall.'

Often learners think that having a question about something is a great excuse to stop working altogether and do nothing until they've captured your undivided attention and extracted an answer from you. The Wonderwall encourages learners to see questions not as roadblocks, but as vehicles to propel them forward. In this context, they can acknowledge their own questions and still see that it is often possible to get on with their work and revisit these questions later.

So, what do we as the teacher do with the Wonderwall? This is where the ingenuity of the resource really begins to shine. Having access into the minds of our learners and seeing what our lessons are making them speculate about is an invaluable gift. We can consult the questions *during* the lesson so that we know whether to adapt our teaching and where to intervene, or we can consult the questions *after* the lesson and use them to inform our planning for the subsequent week. We can even handle Charlie's diverting (but interesting) maths question about whether estimation could be used to calculate the number of acne spots on his back, or Crystal's irrelevant question about why she can't wear hoop earrings, by earnestly allowing them to be posted on the Wonderwall, with a promise that it will be visited in the future.

It doesn't really matter what your Wonderwall looks like – big or small, sticky notes or wipeable surface. As long as it has prominence in your mind, and your teaching, it will be an exciting addition to your classroom. For those of us who don't often teach in a traditional classroom, try using a single clipboard instead. And, if you're lucky enough to have a teaching assistant, consider asking them to circulate during practical work, collecting learners' wondering questions from them and delivering them back to you.

Strategy: Question Metronome

This is another strategy that will get your learners thinking about *asking* questions rather than just regurgitating information or simply waiting around for you to do all the probing.

Divide the class into pairs and ensure that each pair has a recording device on them. Mobile phones are probably the easiest and most readily available option, but if your school has strict rules about the use or presence of mobile phones in lessons you may need to explore other possibilities (the MFL department is often a gold mine for recording equipment, but if they still haven't forgiven you for poaching several of their 'French Café Croissants' last open evening, you may need to look elsewhere …).

Just as a metronome goes back and forth, so will the questions in each pair. You provide the class with a stimulus (e.g. topic, image, problem, word, bank of words) and in one minute learners must rally questions back and forth without pausing. For example, if the stimulus in a PE lesson was an image of a rugby player, the questions generated might sound something like this:

- How is rugby different to football?

- What equipment do you need to play the game?

- Who is the most famous rugby player?

- What numbers play on the front row?

- How did he get so muddy?

- Why do some players get 'cauliflower ears'?

- What is the most common injury rugby players sustain?

- What is a scrum?

- What constitutes a foul in the game?

Once the minute has passed, stop the questioning and have each pair review their recording. They should now perform some analysis of their questions. This can be tailored to the direction you would like to move in next. Perhaps you would like the pairs to jot down questions that are especially interesting and then place them on a Wonderwall (see above) or Wonderball (see Chapter 1). Creating a tick chart which requires them to categorise the types of questions they have been asking could lead to an excellent activity where they build their own challenges or research plans using different levels of questioning. It may even be worthwhile discussing which questions are less useful and why, or which questions are most difficult, or perhaps impossible, to answer. This can also be a fantastic way to lead into writing a narrative piece – instead of brainstorming answers, the collection of questions can facilitate more diverse responses.

Strategy: Question Tokens

To further reinforce just how much you value learners' questions in your classroom, and to encourage them to ask increasingly more of them, give learners Question Tokens that they must 'spend' over the course of the lesson. Their questions can be directed at you or at their classmates during collaborative work. If a learner feels that the question they posed is such a pertinent one that it should be worth two tokens, then they can try to justify why they think this is the case and you can adjudicate. A learner who conscientiously spends all of their tokens, thereby increasing their chances of closing their own learning gaps (and opening up new ones to cross), can be handsomely rewarded in the manner of your choosing (e.g. merits, stamps, notes to parents, house points).

(See also Talk Tokens in Chapter 4.)

Strategy: Prizes for Probing

As an annexe to the Question Tokens strategy, you can simply keep an eager eye out for any great questions that learners might ask during your lesson, and reward them immediately. While you are circulating, listening in to collaborative work, and you hear Rosie pose a brilliant question to the rest of her group about one of the historical sources, seize the opportunity to celebrate this valuable vehicle for potential new learning by awarding an appropriate prize. (This might be a merit, stamp, sticker, etc.) By signalling to the class that you are especially proud of useful questions, you will not only increase the likelihood of more questions being asked, but you will also encourage learners to value their classmates' questions and consider them more deeply.

Of course, one of the most powerful things we can do with questioning in our classrooms is to (gently) interrogate individual learners about their own work. Asking them to explain and justify choices in their writing, art or practical work, or posing just the right question to get them to identify *for themselves* what needs to be improved, is a great way of giving feedback without, well, actually giving it.

For a stack of other ways to give feedback to learners in a way that reduces your output and increases theirs, just turn to Chapter 6.

Chapter 6

Beyond the Red Pen

Progress-Orientated Feedback in the Classroom

Feedback is a vital and incredibly powerful tool in the classroom, but it is important to remember that it is not a magic wand that can simply be pointed at things (or students) to bring about progress. The most important aspect of feedback is creating an ethos for it and then training your learners about how to use it to move themselves forward. It is not something you do *for* them to change their habits; it is something you give *to* them to help them make the changes themselves.

Just like salt on your roast dinner or (as your mother may have warned you) eye make-up on a Friday night, the transformative powers of feedback are great, but they need to be used in moderation. The most important aspect of the feedback we provide, just like the talk we utilise in the classroom, is not to do with quantity. Feedback is at its most effective when it has a cogent focus and a distinct purpose. A clear, precise instruction for upgrading or a carefully targeted development task can get a better result out of learners than the well-meaning half-a-side we sometimes write on a homework submission. In this chapter, we will describe how to streamline feedback to make sure that the advice we give to learners is focused, defined and designed to help them take action.

Despite the fact that feedback plays such an important role in the amount and pace of progress that our learners make, it is unlikely that past pupils will ever stop you in the supermarket to say, 'Mr Jones, I just wanted to say that I always really enjoyed your feedback.' Feedback is not an aspect of our teaching that inherently inspires and it would rarely be classed as enjoyable. Even though it is an aspect of our practice that is often least appreciated and, frustratingly, can be one of the most time-consuming, it is something that we must always strive to get right.

Our feedback has the potential to stretch and empower our learners, but sadly it can also have adverse, demotivating effects if not deployed sensitively. Blind praise without constructive criticism and guidance on how to move forward will never bring about progress for our learners, and instead will instil a false confidence that will likely inhibit subsequent development.

We must also keep in mind that there is an emotional impact any time we find flaw in a piece of work. Let's think about this in the context of a lesson observation, as, professionally, this process is the closest experience for us to the feedback that our learners encounter. You painstakingly prepare a lesson that you feel will go down well with your line manager/senior leadership team/external inspector. Although a little nervous during the delivery, you are really pleased with the way the learners engaged with the material and you know that they made good progress over the course of the lesson. You receive your feedback and the observer comments positively on many aspects of the lesson: they commend your classroom management; they like the displays you have on the walls to support learning; they were very impressed with the ways you deployed your support assistant; the book scrutiny shows that you consistently offer constructive and supportive comments to move learners forward; your resources were pitched just right and really allowed the class to engage in some independent learning; you maintained high expectations for both the individual work they were doing and their participation in the whole-class activities; *but* … you could have provided greater opportunities to stretch and challenge the most able in the class.

So much good, perhaps even outstanding, practice was highlighted in the debrief, but which aspect sticks with you the most? Which comment will you dwell on and hash over and perhaps frontload your response with should anyone ask 'How did your lesson observation go?'? Of course, the one piece of criticism. Does this mean your observer was wrong? Probably not. Does it mean they should have kept this little pearl of wisdom to themselves and allowed you to just feel good about the lesson you delivered? Probably not.

Just as with the formative and summative assessments that we give our learners, receiving feedback on your performance should be a learning opportunity, and if the person providing feedback can't give you some insight into how you can push yourself forward or improve in some capacity, what was the point of their observation? Although an opportunity to have your ego stroked is nice, it is certainly not in the spirit of learning – or, in the case of the lesson observation, professional development.

So, what is the moral of the story? What does the most effective feedback entail? Here are some strategies to ensure you make the biggest impact with your feedback.

Strategy: Build Me Up, Buttercup

While praising that which is not praiseworthy will not facilitate progress, finding success, even if it's small, in the work students have done is vital to making feedback productive. Having confidence in your ability to improve and move forward is essential for learners if they are to make progress, and the best way to foster this is to highlight the skills and abilities they are already displaying and offer guidance on how to build on them. In the event that a catastrophic misconception has occurred and you really struggle to find merit in their attempt, are there any skills or abilities that the learner has displayed proficiency in on previous formative or summative pieces that you can refer to?

Strategy: Identify Gaps That Need Closing

An essential aspect of effective feedback is spotting the gaps in what a learner knows, and doing so with a view to setting goals to close the gaps.

- Can aspects of the work be stretched or improved?

- Are there any vital (or even simply desirable) elements that needed improving?

- Are there any misconceptions or misinformation that needs correcting?

Our role as assessor needs to be to identify these areas for development and either flag them up for the learner in question, or provide a framework to enable learners to address them for themselves in order to move forward.

The identification of any gaps is always most meaningful when they are clearly linked to the objective and success criteria that you share with your learners, so no out-of-nowhere ambushes in your marking! It can be very frustrating for learners to have fault found with an aspect of their work when they were unaware that it would make the piece unsuccessful. For example, if ongoing literacy targets/standards, like spellings, grammar and punctuation, form a part of, or are an addition to, what you are assessing, ensure that you make this clear to your learners in advance. (See Chapter 3 for ideas on making success criteria explicit to your learners.)

Strategy: Set Attainable Challenges In Relation to the Gaps

A key understanding to develop in relation to feedback is that the learning journey is continuous and there is no such thing as perfection. (Except for maybe Reese's Peanut Butter Cups. And Sportacus from *LazyTown*. And the feeling you get on the first day of the summer holidays. But we digress …) No matter what success a learner has with a piece of work, there is always room to stretch, challenge and develop. Even when a piece of work has attained full marks or has met the target level/grade that a learner is aiming for, an additional challenge can always be set to move learning forward. In cases like this, it will likely involve opening up new gaps for learners to address, rather than simply identifying ones that you find within the piece of work in question.

With Great Power Comes Great Responsibility (and a Bit of Time)

This adage is not just about Spiderman's self-awareness. While for Spiderman this was about accepting agency over the impact of his influence, it is more desirable for teachers, in a feedback context, to shuffle the responsibility onto our learners. In order to see measurable results, we need to get our learners to take responsibility for acting on the advice we provide.

The feedback that we give our learners should not always be a top-down dispersal of information, any more than our teaching should. Unless it's a summative assessment piece that learners will have little cause to subsequently engage with, oral or written feedback should be an opportunity for discussion and reflection – not just a final quality stamp on a piece of work.

It's all well and good to have the *expectation* that reflection and action on your comments will happen, but even with the most diligent learners, it's unlikely to occur unless you provide some dedicated time for them to engage with this task. And why shouldn't review and reflection be granted time within the lesson? Acting on the feedback that has been given is a sure-fire way to bring about progress and to make clear to your learners that the skills, knowledge or understanding they are gaining in your class/discipline is a process, not just something they should draw a line under once the piece of work is handed in.

This acting-on-feedback time is best set aside immediately upon receipt of assessed work. Too often learners will have their exercise books or marked assessments returned to them and all they do is skip to the end to see if they were given a house point or merit, glance at the level or grade that has been awarded and go on their merry ways. If they are the competitive sort, they may compare their result with their peers', but the point often gets missed: what have they done really well? What needs a bit of work? What can they do right now to improve this piece of work, close any gaps that are still apparent or stretch the skills they demonstrated?

The time you allocate to this important task may simply be 10 minutes at the outset of the lesson to respond to your questions, make simple corrections and/or address any ongoing literacy targets that need attention. Alternatively, for more substantial pieces of work, you may want to devote a whole lesson to developing skills in line with feedback as learners embark on redrafting or extending a piece of work.

The following strategies will lend some shape and structure to your acting-on-feedback time.

Strategy: The Gap Task

Providing a Gap Task as a part of your written feedback is an excellent way to personalise the targets and action points you set for your learners. The Gap Task involves setting your learners a personalised mission with reference to the work they've done – a task that seeks to close the gaps that are evident in their skills, knowledge or understanding. Some learners find it frustrating to be asked to go back and redo aspects of a piece of work that have not been wholly successful – the Gap Task gives them an opportunity to explore the same skills with a fresh task, but to approach it this time around with your feedback and the 'mistakes' they made the first time in mind. As mentioned before, the Gap Task may be designed to help the learner address shortcomings in prior attempts or it may be a tailored task aimed at stretching them further, thus opening a new gap for them to cross.

Setting Gap Tasks need not be a time-consuming or onerous undertaking. It can be as simple as a one-line question or sentence detailing what you would like them to do to evidence their progress in relation to your feedback. Invariably, when we mark a whole set of books, common faults emerge, so it may be appropriate to create, for example, six Gap Tasks and simply indicate which task you would like each of your learners to undertake.

The purpose of the Gap Task is not to bring in new information or skills, but rather to ensure that the understanding intended through a specific piece of work is secure, and that any areas for development that you identify through your marking and feedback can be addressed proactively.

Strategy: My Turn, Your Turn

This strategy is an effective means to ensure that learners are engaging in, and understanding, the comments and feedback that you provide in assessing their work. It creates a middle-ground for self-assessment and teacher-led assessment. My Turn, Your Turn can be approached in two different ways:

1   The teacher can provide annotations in the body of the work and the learner uses these annotations to create a summative comment that highlights best practice and sets targets for areas that need development and/or further scrutiny.

2   The teacher provides a summative comment that highlights best practice from the work and identifies areas for development. The learner then needs to scrutinise the work to find evidence of best practice and any aspects that require further attention.

From a progress perspective, this process makes it very clear to the learner what they have been successful at and where further concentration would be best directed. If there are any aspects of the feedback that have been unclear, they will need to query them in order to complete the task. Inviting this kind of discussion around feedback and development is important. Learners need to understand that they should not just blindly accept the targets they are given, but rather ensure that they actually know what they mean!

This type of strategy means the responsibility for reflection on a piece of work is shared. Learners will need training and modelling to carry out this task effectively, but supporting the close scrutiny of feedback raises the profile of the comments you provide and forces learners to think qualitatively about what your observations mean. Once established as a routine, this will also undoubtedly impact on their ability to perform self-assessment and peer assessment positively.

Strategy: The Autopsy Pen

Using an 'Autopsy Pen' makes the revisions learners undertake (as a result of feedback) highly visible. Learners perform a 'post-mortem' on their work by using a designated colour to comment on, alter or add to their assessed piece of work. This works best when a common 'autopsy' colour is used across the class. It needs to be different from the colour that the teacher uses so that learners' adaptations are clearly differentiated.

In this way, progress on the piece of work is highly visible to any stakeholder who looks at the learners' work – it is clear how and where learners are acting upon advice and feedback. The most important stakeholder in this process is always the learner, for whom these clear steps forward should be very motivating. For the class teacher, it becomes much easier (and more timely) to see what revisions have been made and if any further attention or comment is required. For any other stakeholders, such as parents or friendly book-scrutinisers, making obvious this routine of improving work and refining skills is beneficial as it can guide any conversations they have about the learners' progress and understanding. The ritual use of an Autopsy Pen makes plain the emphasis that you as the class teacher place on getting it *right* rather than just getting it *done*.

Strategy: Production Line for Progress

Developing the skills required for peer assessment is vital for making it a meaningful and worthwhile process. Our learners are not inherently skilled at giving constructive feedback, especially when they themselves are not experts in the skill they are developing. The Production Line for Progress is a great way to model for learners the processes involved in peer assessment, and to let them gain experience of this form of assessment in a structured and supervised context.

Work is peer assessed as on a production line: each learner receives a piece of their classmates' work and you provide a block of time for them to reflect on this work using specific success criteria. It is important to provide a sharp focus for their reflection as we all know that peer support can be unhelpful if learners are not given strict parameters for their comments (e.g. 'Your handwriting is cool …'). The focus should always be linked to the lesson objective and success criteria agreed for the piece of work, otherwise confusion will ensue.

Once the block of time (two or three minutes) has lapsed, the learner passes the piece of work they have been assessing one person to the right and, in turn, receives one piece of work from the left. They then resume the assessment process on the new piece of work. It can be helpful if learners create a marking 'key' to reflect who has contributed which comments and ideas. This keeps learners accountable and allows you to chase up anything that emerges from the marking. Learners can simply start from where the first person left off or they could start from the beginning and add additional comments or catch errors the first person missed.

This can also work well if the assessor is given a different focus with each exchange they make. So, if the first peer marker is searching for correct usage of key terms, the second could be looking for examples of fact and opinion, and the third may be marking for spelling, punctuation and grammar. You can allow for as many exchanges of the work as you feel is purposeful.

This production line serves several purposes: not only are learners receiving guided feedback on which they can reflect, but they are also given the opportunity to see how a variety of their peers have approached the task, potentially picking up ideas of best practice along the way.

Strategy: Feedback Time Capsule

Prompt feedback ensures that learners are able to effectively reflect on their developing skills and understanding. But how do we keep learners accountable for longer-term targets that result from formative and summative pieces? Do they even remember what knowledge, skills and understanding they have acquired from topic to topic, and which skills are secure versus those that require attention? In Key Stage 2 and beyond, learners will often track specific targets in their exercise books and should always be aware of the level or grade they are working at and the level or grade they are targeted. However, these goals are not always made time-sensitive in an explicit way.

The concept of a time capsule may be a helpful one in order to give learners the opportunity to reflect on what they need to achieve and give them set intervals at which to consider their progress and potential next course of action. After receiving feedback on an assessed piece of work, learners identify their greatest areas of success in relation to this specific piece and the areas that still require development. This is then extended to asking learners to predict where they will be in relation to these targets by the time the next summative assessment (or other designated time interval) is reached. It is also useful for them to suggest action points about how this will be done and/or what success might look like. This forms the learners' contribution to the time capsule.

When the time interval has lapsed, return the entries to the class and have them reflect on where they are in relation to where they thought they would be. Was the target useful? If they have not met the target, has it held back any particular aspect of their wider performance? If not, was the target a useful one? If it wasn't, how can they seek to rectify it? Have more significant areas of development emerged in the meantime? How have they continued to use the areas of best practice that were identified? Have they developed these skills?

It is easy for learners to forget the journey they've been on over the course of an academic year, so reflective opportunities like the Feedback Time Capsule can be a good way to remind them of where they've been and the progress they've made in their learning journey. Success or failure in meeting the targets set should not necessarily be rewarded or punished. Instead, the opportunity for learners to consider how they utilise and develop the skills and abilities they acquire over the course of the year should be embraced.

Try This ...   CPD

Why not consider a continuing professional development (CPD) time capsule? So often we attend a training day or course and come back buzzing with ideas, thinking 'I can try that!', and within a week we've forgotten much of what has been said. This is not out of laziness – it's likely to be because more immediate pressures take over and we simply never get around to it.

After a course or INSET you have enjoyed, make two separate lists:

1. Two things you want to try yourself and two things you would like to share with colleagues in the next week.

2. Any other ideas from the course that you want to try, tweak in your practice or share with others.

Make the items on your first list a priority and try them out right away. It is important to share ideas that you know will benefit colleagues while they are fresh in your mind and you are feeling enthusiastic. It is sensible to start with manageable targets that you will be able to integrate smoothly into your routine. Try to alter too much at once and it is unlikely you will have success with them all and you will probably revert back to the exact same practice you had before.

The second list will form your time capsule. No one is suggesting you should bury it in the car park or school playground! Rather that you put it away for a chosen period of time – this may be a fortnight, a month or a term – and then revisit the ideas you were hoping to test out and the changes you hoped to have made. If you use a paper planner, attach the list to the relevant future page or make a note on that date to dig out your list and analyse your progress. If you plan electronically, set a reminder for yourself instead.

When you examine your list, evaluate how you got on with the two initial changes you wished to implement. Are you still using them? How have you changed the idea to make it your own? Are there items on your list that you still have left to try? Have the changes you had hoped to make come to fruition? Is there anything that you would like to revisit?

Any training that we receive is only as good as what we do with it. Keeping it at the forefront of our minds is difficult when our job moves at the pace that it does!

Time Is of the Essence

A widely accepted tenet of effective feedback is that it is most valuable when delivered in a timely fashion. This is common sense: learners' ability to remember the reasons why they completed the task in the way they did will be more acute if they receive feedback sooner rather than later. If they can recall the thought processes and explicit teaching that went into the first attempt, they will be able to act on advice and potential revisions much more proficiently. There is no golden threshold about the amount of time that lapses between learners finishing a piece of work and receiving feedback and its efficacy in helping them to make progress. However, especially when you are expecting learners themselves to review and revise the piece of work, it is important to allow them to revisit the work as soon as possible so that the skills you are asking them to refine do not become muddled with new learning. (Most of us know how irritating it can be when, for example, we are observed teaching and then have to wait several days before we get any feedback about our lesson.)

Nevertheless, there is a distinct difference between *timely* feedback and *immediate* feedback. While it is most useful for learners to receive advice and assessment of their work promptly, this does not mean that they should receive it immediately at all stages throughout its composition and then directly afterwards. It is important to ensure that learners have time to reflect on and engage with their own work before it is handed over to someone else to assess – be it their class teacher, support assistant or peer.

> **If learners are not given an opportunity to consider their own work before getting feedback on it, they will soon learn to rely on feedback – becoming feedback junkies who depend on their next 'fix' to get on with the task at hand.**

Of course, formative comments (often verbal) to support learners in revising their work as it develops are apt, as long as learners are also provided with sufficient time to consider their own work before it is assessed by someone else. Consider the following technique as a way to help support verbal formative feedback.

Strategy: Verbal Feedback Stamp

There is no quicker, more personalised and timelier form of feedback than that which we can provide orally. This is one of the most valuable and powerful types of teacher-talk. Unlike written feedback, learners can request immediate clarification if your advice doesn't make sense to them. As teacher, our verbal feedback during a lesson can intercept misconceptions before a piece of work is finished and submitted. Sage advice on how to best complete a piece of work and/or avoid common mistakes can be directed to relevant groups of learners. The obvious shortcoming of verbal feedback, however, is that as soon as you have said it, it's gone. There is no record of it or much opportunity to reflect on it later. For this reason, it's difficult to make learners accountable for that feedback later.

A verbal feedback stamp is just the solution for this problem. This little gem can be easily procured from a number of places online and, during circulation, is a perfect way to create a record on learners' written work that a conversation was held about the work in question. The following proviso, however, is extremely important: to make the evidence meaningful, create a routine for your learners that when you stamp their work with the verbal feedback stamp, they must immediately jot down brief bullet points detailing the action points from the conversation you've just had.

The learners' next step must then be to act upon that advice. Including this as a part of your progress-oriented feedback routine makes learners more accountable for the verbal advice you give them (and eliminates the necessity to repeat the observations when you mark the finished product!).

Marking: The Greatest Time-Thief of All

Ask any teacher what the greatest obstacle in providing their learners with the very best progress-oriented feedback is, and you will almost unanimously get the same response: time. As a profession, teaching has the ability to place inordinate demands on our time. If we completed every aspect of our job in the most thorough fashion possible, we would likely be forced to take up residence in the classroom stationery cupboard because there would be no time to ever leave school. Marking can be a particular challenge – as any teacher dejectedly toting home a mountain of marking on an evening will testify. The key to striking the right home–work balance is to ensure that the feedback you are providing is sharply focused to the learning objective and is progress-oriented. You can save your ink on any other superfluous comments about generic features of the work that you might have felt compelled to write.

The following strategies will give you some ideas for streamlining the process of marking.

Write-Less Marking

- Arm yourself with a highlighter and draw a box around the paragraph/section of work you would most like the learner to reflect on. List focused clear revisions that you expect the learner to act upon *in that targeted section only*.

- Before they submit their work, ask learners to annotate it, identifying the aspects they deem as the most important/challenging/confusing. It may be helpful to provide them with sentence stems such as:
  - I did this because …
  - I'm not sure if this is correct because …
  - This challenged me because …
  - This is my favourite bit because …
  - I used [skill/strategy] here to show …

● [Name of peer/resource] helped me with this part.

Should full sentences like these feel too cumbersome or time-consuming, create a key for the main self-assessment phrases you would like them to use so that learners just have to fill in the details. Once this is completed, your marking can focus on responding to the learner's own annotations.

■ After completing formative written work, ask learners to underline what they perceive to be their best idea (linked to success criteria, key skills, lesson objective, etc.). Also ask them to underline (in a different colour) part of the work that they feel they could develop further. Focus your feedback on these two ideas. Getting learners to think about what they could have improved before they even submit their work is a great way to train them in the important routine of proofreading.

■ At the end of a written task, ask learners to write down a question that they still have about the task or topic. In your feedback, suggest a resource that will assist them in finding the answer or practising the skill rather than answering it for them.

■ It can be onerous to mark *all* aspects of literacy, in addition to subject-based skills, and it can be disheartening for learners to see masses of corrections. This may put them off of taking on valuable skills-based advice or cause them to miss the praise you have given. Choose one (maybe two) literacy focuses that you will correct when marking and make sure that learners are made aware of this before they complete the work. When marking, only focus on learners' use of these key skills (e.g. capital letters, spelling of key words, use of paragraphs) in addition to your feedback on the task itself.

■ If you do need to provide feedback on grammar, punctuation and spelling, highlight literacy mistakes in the first paragraph only. On returning the work to them, get learners to count the number of corrections in the first paragraph and work on an assumption that there will be approximately the same number to find in the following paragraphs. Learners should then set about finding these mistakes and correcting them themselves.

■ Obviously, it is not only *attainment* that is important. Consider using a key to indicate holistically your overall impression of the *effort* learners have put into the piece of work. The following is useful:

✓+ (tick plus) Excellent work – you have surpassed expectations

✓ (tick) Good work – you have met expectations

✓– (tick minus) You have completed the bare minimum (learners with this designation may need to expand or redraft parts of their work)

R (redo) Unacceptable effort – work needs to be reattempted

Of course, comments on effort are always a subjective appraisal that will need to be coupled with observation of learners' working habits, in addition to the written product. Providing a quick assessment like this removes the time-consuming need to write a comment like, 'I can see you have worked hard on this, well done' or 'Too much chatting in lesson, you have not spent enough time on this', and it creates an ongoing record of their working habits in class.

■ Highlight three things in green that successfully meet the objective and highlight one thing in red that needs improving. Learners must infer from this what they have done well and what their target should be, and record this accordingly. (See also My Turn, Your Turn above.)

Strategy: Marking Symbols

Even very young children can be encouraged to respond actively to written feedback on their work. While they may not be able to understand a teacher's written comments, they can easily interpret a clear symbol, especially if you have explicitly shared a custom-designed set of symbols with them beforehand.

This is easiest to do after you have identified the frequently occurring errors across the work of an entire class and can therefore determine what relevant targets you might set. Once you have done this, you can assign a simple, relevant symbol to each target and then share the meaning of these with the class when you hand back their marked work. A list of symbols might look something like this:

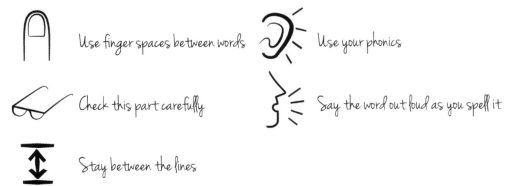

Use finger spaces between words

Use your phonics

Check this part carefully

Say the word out loud as you spell it

Stay between the lines

As long as the learners understand the significance of your chosen symbols, they should be able to respond by improving the work where you have used the symbols or by acting on their personal targets in the subsequent task.

Of course, the simpler you make your symbols, the easier they are to produce freehand as you mark. Or you could push the boat out and invest in a set of stamps!

While marking may not erode your voice, it can certainly be a task that can erode your weekends and evenings. By using the strategies in this chapter, however, you should begin to see not only your marking paying off in a more visible way, but also that dreaded pile of marking shrinking more quickly as your learners play a bigger role in identifying their own weaknesses and setting and managing their own targets.

Chapter 7

Stepping Off Your Soapbox

Using Peer Teaching to Maximise Progress

Still struggling to break those metaphorical chains that keep you bound to the front of your classroom? Those manacles that stop you weaving among the kids and that make it so much harder for you to get real feedback about the gains that individuals in your classroom are making? This is the habit that has us feeling that we're doing too much of the work for our learners, and that allows our learners to come to expect to have things done *for* them and learning done *to* them.

And let's face it, feeling reliant on someone else to do a big chunk of the work for you is not even a satisfying feeling. If you've ever experienced one of the following situations in your time, you'll know what we're talking about:

- You're struggling with your homework but your mum thinks it looks so interesting that she does questions 3, 4 and 5 for you.

- You're working on a still-life painting and your art teacher comes over, takes your brush and adds a load of expert shading and definition.

- Your dad constructs your Lego spaceship while you're in bed.

- You beat your grandad at chess and then discover he's let you win.

- Your sister finishes that page of the colouring book you were working on.

Learners don't walk away from situations like this with a sense of accomplishment and pride (and nor should the perpetrators!).

In this chapter, it truly is time to step away from that imaginary lectern, resist all the temptations to fly in and prevent learners from getting stuck, and refrain from propping up learners in such a way that they will fall the moment you disappear out of the picture. It's time to cash in on that common-sense way of elevating understanding: *peer teaching*.

Think about it. Once you have learnt something new (a skill or some information), as soon as you explain or 'teach' this to another person, one of two things happens: you may begin to feel your own understanding of the concept become more profound and 'cloudless'; or, in attempting to explain the concept, you realise there are elements on which you still require further clarity.

You may have experienced this feeling when forced to put your own ideas down in writing too. It is the obligation to articulate in words the concept or skill, which has hitherto existed non-verbally in our consciousness, that suddenly forces a more precise understanding of it.

Try This ...

CPD

Try explaining the following education-related terms to someone who can't see the list. You shouldn't use the terms themselves or derivations of them.

- Academic
- Pedagogy
- Intervention
- Community cohesion

Were there any that you struggled to define, despite the fact that you had initially felt confident about its meaning?

Did you notice your understanding of any of the terms sharpen as you worked hard to explain them in your own words?

Peer teaching comes in all kinds of forms. But it doesn't call for miniature mortarboards and it certainly doesn't require a military operation to make it an easy and natural part of any lesson. Since the very essence of peer teaching is learners explaining concepts or demonstrating skills to one another, it's easy to see how a great many of the strategies already covered in this book naturally encompass an element of peer teaching.

What's more, during activities which put the lion's share of the work back onto the learners, the teacher is freed up to circulate, listen to the learning and indulge in that really valuable type of teacher-talk – personalised, targeted, one-on-one interactions with individuals.

So, read on for a host of strategies that will free you up to work the room and maximise learners' progress by helping them to do a little bit of the teaching too!

Strategy: Looking for Links

This activity can be used to explore the relationships between various elements of your topic. The task requires each individual to be holding something which relates to the topic you are studying (e.g. an object, word, picture, phrase, number – see the examples below). Tell the learners that on your signal they must get up and circulate with their item, speaking to as many classmates as possible with a view to establishing as many meaningful links as they can between what they are holding and what their classmate is holding.

Learners should carefully scrutinise each other's items and avoid dismissing the possibility of a connection too quickly. If appropriate, you might also encourage them to consider further connections than simply the initial one that pops into their mind. Each interaction will require learners to explain to each other what they perceive the links and relationships to be between the impromptu pairings. Genres of text or art can be linked through noticing common features, images can be linked with words, objects can be linked through their use and so on.

In some instances, there may be specific links that you are hoping for them to spot, while in other lessons it may be a more open task where the learners explore a limitless number of possible connections. The following examples demonstrate the true versatility of this task.

Give half the class ...	and the other half ...	and ask them to ...
A single grade each (e.g. A–, B+, D) and, if appropriate, the grade descriptor too	An anonymous sample of work	Consider which pieces of work match with which grade and how they know
Photocopies of a teacher's written comments – a different comment for each learner – taken from yours or a colleague's marking	Excerpts of learners' work	Debate which comments might match which pieces of work, and why
Objects, quotes or concepts from the topic	The categories that these items could fit into	Consider which items might fit into which categories, and justify their decisions
A word each	A word each	Link up according to: ■ Phonics ■ Meaning ■ Theme ■ Category
An image each	An image each	Link up according to: ■ Genre ■ Emotion ■ Medium ■ Message ■ Target audience

Give half the class ...	and the other half ...	and ask them to ...
Their own completed piece of work	Their own completed piece of work	Look for similarities and differences between the two pieces of work. For very young children, this might be something simple like 'we both used the big paintbrush', and for older learners it could be a sophisticated analysis of each other's work against certain success criteria. A great magpie opportunity!
A quotation or assertion	A fictional character, historical figure or religion	Match up, either from memory, or with the help of the relevant text
Causes	Effects or consequences	Match up and explain the reason or process
Key terms or sight words	Corresponding images, definitions or translations	Link up correctly, exchange cards with someone else and then find their next perfect match, and so on
Pertinent points (e.g. in an essay)	Examples of evidence to support the points (textual or pictorial)	Consider which evidence would best support which points and explain why

Give half the class ...	and the other half ...	and ask them to ...
Fractions	Decimals or percentages	Match up and explain their working out
A number or sum each	A number or sum each	Explore the relationships between them
Names or pictures of animals	Corresponding habitats/ features or food of animals	Link up accurately, exchange cards with someone else and then find their next perfect match, and so on

Looking for Links can be used as an introductory task – to gain information about current levels of understanding, and again later on – after new learning has occurred, to explore what fresh connections learners can now make that were not apparent to them previously.

For the youngest learners, it can be helpful to scaffold the activity by asking them to sit down as soon as they have made a connection to avoid losing focus on the task. Once you have called on a few pairings to share their findings, challenge them to find an alternative connection.

Strategy: Mallett's Mallet

If you are old enough to have watched Saturday morning television in the 1980s (sigh) or old enough to have watched your kids watch it (double sigh), then you'll have a good idea of what we're talking about here. Timmy Mallett made this activity famous as part of a TV show, but adapted for the classroom it can be an excellent vehicle to help learners realise that they can be self-reliant, that they do have a starting point and that they don't need to immediately default to asking the teacher the moment they feel stuck.

Assuming your classroom cupboard isn't conveniently full of mallets (we hope it's not), you will need some balloons for this. Learners sit in pairs with a balloon placed between them and a pen each. Let them know that they will be working in a competitive context and within a time limit. Your job is to reveal or announce a series of concepts or questions related to the topic. For example, if you were preparing learners to write a descriptive piece about a football game you might say, 'Things you would see at a football game!' or 'Things you would smell at a football game', or even 'Types of moves in football!' If you were preparing them for an exam question on Judaism, you might say 'Jewish artefacts!', 'Jewish beliefs!' or 'Jewish customs!'

In their pairs, the learners must rapidly take it in turns to write down a relevant response to create one long list. If one of them thinks that the other person has hesitated for too long or that their contribution is not apt, then they bop their partner on the head with the balloon (in a 'Little Rabbit Foo Foo' way – not a 'Wreck-It Ralph' way!).

The more you use this strategy, the more effective it becomes in helping learners to draw out the knowledge they do have deep down, but which sometimes needs a metaphorical crowbar to extract it. Consider, for example, the following prompt: 'Facts about the Tudors!' Now, some of you may at first think to yourselves, 'Oh, darn it. I'm not a history teacher. I only remember covering the Romans and the Egyptians at school. I have no starting point. I'm done for.' However, placed in this competitive context, and with the clock ticking, you soon discover that actually you know two – no, several – no, *many* things about the Tudors. You will probably end up excavating titbits like these from your mind:

- Henry VIII was King of England and he had six wives.

- One of them was called Anne Boleyn.

- He had her head chopped off.

- Kings were able to have people beheaded!

- Shakespeare wrote plays during that time.

- People went to the theatre!

- They built houses with beams showing on the outside.

- They wore ruffs.

- And stripey tights.

OK, so you may have had to rely on your familiarity with *Blackadder* there a little, but the point is, the task – with all its sense of urgency and competition – has taken you from a point of, 'Oh gosh, I don't know!' to 'I already have nine things I can tell you about the Tudors!' The other beneficial outcome of this approach is that the responses your partner provides can spark off more of your own ideas.

Once they have generated their list, the pairs can be encouraged to pick out particularly good ideas and jettison others. You might even ask them to sort the contributions into categories or share their list with an adjacent pair. Of course, what you have now is a room-ful of lists which can be used in various ways as a valuable resource for a subsequent piece of work!

It's easy to see how this simple little activity, if used regularly, can train learners into realising that they do have some kind of starting point. It's especially useful for learners who, despite having been taught a concept extremely well, still maintain that they're stuck. This feigned helplessness is often rooted in a profound lack of confidence in their own ability as a learner. So, next time a learner tells you they're stuck, don't rush in and save the day – tell them to turn to their partner and do a quick round of Mallett's Mallet – with or without the balloon!

Learning that they can make a start without your input is an extremely important lesson for many learners. It can be useful to use this technique frequently in the run-up to an exam. In this way, you can point out to learners that if they feel a 'blank page' moment coming on when they stare at that exam question, they only have to imagine that they are playing Mallett's Mallet with someone. They will quickly find that they can produce a list of ideas which they can then use as hooks on which to hang their written response.

Strategy: Paparazzi Pupils

An important aspect of effective peer teaching is securing learners' understanding of what constitutes a good piece of work. Paparazzi Pupils raises learners' awareness of what represents excellent practice and requires them to identify and explore it.

Choose two or three learners to be your Paparazzi Pupils. (Whenever you use this strategy, choose individuals whom you feel will most benefit from gaining a better grasp of what good practice looks like and will make gains from observing the work of others.) Give your paparazzi team digital cameras and get them to circulate in the classroom, searching for and capturing examples of excellent work. This technique works especially well in a practical lesson, but photographers can also take close-up shots of written work.

At an opportune point in the lesson, display the images and ask the photographers to justify their choices. Get the class as a whole to discuss what makes these examples great, or if anything could be done to improve them.

In this way, you are enabling learners to explicitly articulate the features of excellent work, as well as magpie all kinds of quality ideas from the best examples in the class. As an extension, you can print off the images and ask learners to analyse and annotate them – stating specifically where they excel or fall short of expectations.

Strategy: Jigsaw

A great way to make every learner feel that they have an integral part to play in the lesson is to use this ingenious method of group mixing. Called Jigsaw because the end result involves all the 'pieces' coming together, this strategy can be used extremely successfully for introducing a measured amount of new information or for revising a topic fully and quickly.

The technique is used in two separate stages of a lesson and is best explained with the help of the diagram below:

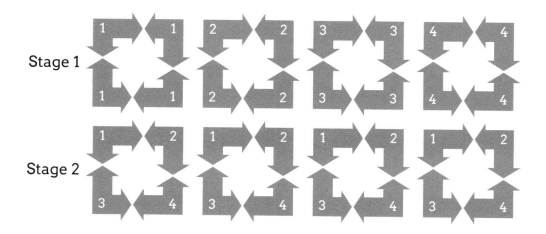

In the first stage of the lesson, learners operate from within 'expert groups'. Each group will work on becoming experts in a certain aspect of a topic. In other words, with reference to the diagram above, all the 1s might be given information about Victorian *dress* and are expected to scrutinise the information together and become the class authorities on this subject. In the meantime, the 2s might be becoming experts in the area of Victorian *food*, the 3s in the area of Victorian *schooling* and so on.

While this first stage might involve the learners perusing information that you have given them, it could equally involve them researching the subject themselves, via books or the internet. During stage 1, as well as becoming impressively clued-up in their designated sections of the topic, the groups of learners should also be planning and rehearsing together how they intend to relay this information to their other classmates in stage 2.

The next stage of the activity requires the learners to move into mixed groups. This means that, within the new groups, each section of the topic will be represented by just one expert. It is now the job of each learner to share their expertise in turn, carefully teaching the key information to the other learners in their group. Once each learner has taken their turn to communicate the information they reviewed in stage 1, you should end up with a situation where every learner can consider themselves an expert in all the other topic areas too.

It's easy to see how this strategy can allow you to take a relatively large topic and effectively disseminate all the relevant information across the whole class, without bending learners' ears with excessive teacher-talk. It can, of course, work equally well for teaching a practical skill – for example, a series of movements in a gymnastics display or consecutive sections of a recorder recital.

As with the strategies in Chapter 2, this activity prevents any learner from being a passenger. The Jigsaw requires every single participant to work hard and efficiently, because they must each deliver their crucial part of the jigsaw effectively in order for the entire class to move forward in understanding together. A real sense of accountability and responsibility is a natural side effect of taking part in the strategy.

Another fabulous strategy for helping learners to effectively and efficiently teach each other is Teach Me, Tell Me (and Then Tell Me More!) (see Chapter 8 for a full explanation of this genius technique). As with Jigsaw, Tell Me More enables learners to spread and embed an enormous amount of information in a relatively short period of time without you even needing to open your mouth!

Everyday Value

No, we're not talking about supermarket basics. We're referring to the unarguable value of fostering learners' self-belief and self-reliance every day – not just now and again. But this doesn't mean we should expect learners to be naturally independent and, therefore, independent work to be naturally productive. As discussed in Chapter 2, many learners, when suddenly expected to learn autonomously, will accomplish very little, especially if they have had a lot of experience of being spoon-fed previously.

There is a huge chasm between doing most of the hard work for our learners and just leaving them to fend for themselves. When we teach our children to ride a bike, for example, we don't just sit them on the saddle, declare 'Off you go!' and send them hurtling down a hill. We give them stabilisers to bridge the gap between reliance and independence.

Like stabilisers, there are some support systems that we can put in place in our classrooms that become, in the learners' eyes, a natural, supportive part of every lesson. These systems require learners to actively seek and assimilate information, to regularly review and consolidate skills, and to recognise that their first port of call can be their very own selves.

Strategy: The Enable Table

Allocate a table somewhere in the classroom where you can place resources that will act as a supplement to the core resources and help to stretch the most able and support the least able. (If you're teaching outside or in a room with no tables, substitute this with a special box in which you can place the relevant items.)

Examples of the types of items you might place on your Enable Table include:

- Definitions of complex vocabulary

- 'Wow' words you would like learners to use

- Prompts or questions to get learners thinking

- Examples of aspirational work

- Dictionaries and thesauruses

- Information sheets

■ A list of 'success steps'

■ A checklist for learners who think they've finished

■ Exciting extension tasks (these should always be of an irresistible nature so learners don't feel that working hard and finishing early results in punishing 'extra work')

■ A model answer showing the working-out process

■ Hints or clues

Tell your learners that they may access the Enable Table at their own discretion. Explain that every one of them will need to make use of the table from time to time. Sometimes this might be because they feel stuck and want to seek out inspiration to get started, some ideas to build up their work or an explanation of an element they find tricky. Sometimes it might be because they have completed their work and want to take on a 'challenge task'. Or perhaps they want to pick up some pointers about how to improve what they have already done. There is no shame in using the Enable Table.

What's more, it is a very visible approach to differentiation – a strategy which signals to the learners that you understand that they are a class of individuals with varying needs. You should avoid placing duplicated resources on your Enable Table – learners should not be allowed to pick up a sheet and take it back to their table, as this may prevent them from assimilating and thinking about the information. Instead, they should be encouraged to peruse the material at the Enable Table and bring the pertinent information back inside their heads.

Strategy: Peer Appointments

Sometimes you just need learners to complete individual, focused work while you circulate, offering help and guidance. You can, however, still sprinkle the power of peer teaching into these lessons by organising structured, timely opportunities for learners to 'meet up' and discuss their work. Scheduling special appointment times for pairs of learners to get together may be a new concept for your class, but it can add a great sense of intrigue and anticipation to the lesson. It can also break up long periods of individual work in a useful and controlled way.

When you first introduce this strategy, it's best if you to coordinate the appointments quite strictly. This is when you get to behave like the officious receptionist at your local medical centre! At the beginning of the lesson, tell the learners who their appointment partner is and at what time their meeting will take place. (Initially you may find it easiest to schedule everyone's appointment during the same five-minute slot in the middle of the lesson, so that all the meetings begin and end at the same time.)

The purpose of the appointments is for learners to share their work and ask for advice on how to improve. (Clearly your choice of pairings is important, so select pairs carefully and be sure to stick close to those you think may struggle to support each other effectively.) Learners should be encouraged to ask questions about each other's work, and if there is a point that they are both unsure about, they should consult you. A checklist can help pairs to unpick and assess each other's work effectively (see Chapter 3). An allocation of five minutes for the meeting is usually a good amount of time to instil a sense of urgency and keep the conversation on task.

Knowing that their appointment time is looming is an effective way of motivating learners to work efficiently and with that all-important target audience in mind. Having a very real designated reader in their sights as they work encourages them to write clearly and purposefully.

Strategy: Progress Wall

In the same way as a Wonderwall (Chapter 5) is designed to collect questions and support a culture of wondering in the classroom, the Progress Wall tracks progress and gains made in relation to both short-term and long-term objectives.

Simply take a blank display board and cover it with pale-coloured paper that can be easily written on. Tell the class that this is their Progress Wall for the current topic and that every time a key learning point is covered or somebody contributes a brilliant point to the class discussion, you or they will be marking it up on the board. If you 'grow' your Progress Wall from left to right, learners can clearly see that their learning growing too. In other words, a few lessons into the topic, you will have a small section of the wall covered; by the middle of your unit of work, you will see half the wall covered; by the end you will have an entire wall full of all the admirable progress that has been made!

You might use the Progress Wall to record key terms, important questions with answers that have been discovered through enquiry by the class, images or photos that demonstrate the progress that has been made on a specific topic or unit, or to display marked work. Creating the Progress Wall with your class is a fantastic way of visibly showing your learners (in a very explicit way) what they are learning and participating in over the course of a unit.

The Progress Wall can also be used as a resource for reminding learners about key concepts that they should be familiar with when they embark on an independent assignment. Having a place in the classroom where they can access help, without defaulting to asking the class teacher or support assistant, is a great way to encourage greater independence in their working habits. The fact that they have played a part in the creation of the Progress Wall, as opposed to displays that are entirely teacher-created, is important for self-esteem and a sense of ownership.

The Progress Wall can also be an excellent tool for learners who have missed a lesson or series of lessons. (You know, those learners who ask you, 'Did you do anything important while I was away?') You can simply direct that learner to the Progress Wall to discover (or at least formulate some questions about) what has been added in their absence. This puts some of the onus back onto the learner for catching up on missed work. Although they will likely need to come to you for clarification and specific assignments, they will at least have taken the first steps in identifying some of the ideas and concepts they need to find out about.

Try This ...

Make your Progress Wall an easily-moveable feature (e.g. use drawing pins or pressure-sensitive adhesive rather than staples). In this way, you can quickly change your displays for different classes or different topics. You can also take them off the wall, store them and get them back out for revision at a later date. If you have an interactive whiteboard, you can use the 'Save a page' facility to create a digital Progress Wall.

Passing the Impasse

Sometimes learners will reach a point in their work where they feel they can't move on. They feel thoroughly stuck, as if they've reached a dead end in their understanding, inspiration or motivation. In fact, let's face it, some of our learners can even *begin* tasks in this frame of mind. Hell, sometimes they'll even *enter our classrooms* in that frame of mind.

In these circumstances, clear, well-embedded self-help routines are an absolute must. Learners should have a good understanding of what to do if they feel they have reached an impasse, so that pockets of unproductivity don't develop in your classroom. More importantly, you need to give learners some self-support strategies so that you don't end up navigating a sea of learners with their hands in the air waiting to ask you questions like, 'Should I turn to the next page now, Miss?' or 'Can I use my jumbo novelty pencil?'

Well-known popular classroom routines such as 3B4Me and the 4B's are extremely useful in helping learners to be more self-reliant, and can completely change the way your lessons unfold. For those of you who are not yet converts, these strategies involve giving learners three instructions to follow before they default to sticking their hand in the air and asking you to sort it out for them or declaring that they're stuck:

Instructions for Learners

Step 1: Re-consult your own brain. Yes, that's right – stop and think again. Read your own work carefully. For many of the questions that get asked in lessons, just thinking a little bit harder about them will let you realise that you do, in fact, know the answer. Stay calm and think it through carefully – you may well be able to use common sense to work it out.

Step 2: If you've re-consulted your own brain and you're still stuck then you need to consult a resource. This might be a classroom display – have a look to see if there is something on the wall that could help you. Check the whiteboard again for instructions and information. Have a look back through your notes from previous lessons. Read the textbook or worksheet carefully. Look in a dictionary or a thesaurus. If appropriate, Google it!

Step 3: If you've taken both of the steps above, and you still don't have a solution for your problem, then you can ask a classmate – see if they can help you with your question.

These three preliminary steps can eliminate a lot of the problems before they even reach your busy ears. They also help learners to start recognising how some of their queries are actually unnecessary or time-wasting. They teach learners that they have the resources within themselves to solve problems and find answers. Only if learners have taken all three steps can they bring their problem to you. If it does reach this point in the process, then it is far more likely that the problem will be a valid one, and you can assist accordingly.

It may be that you want to designate particular learners who can be consulted during step 3. These 'consultants' might be chosen for a number of reasons – because of their expertise, because you want to raise their self-esteem, because you want to reward them with

a sense of responsibility, because they steamed through the first task and so on. If you want to make this strategy very high profile, you can sit your consultants at the Enable Table (see above). Your consultants should, of course, have their own work to get on with when they're not engaging in the beneficial activity of peer teaching! You might want to consider giving your consultants a resource they can refer to that will help them to support their peers even more efficiently.

Try This ...

The next time you've set a task where a minority of learners finish successfully while you're still racing around trying to support the learners who are struggling, here's what you can do. Each time a learner successfully completes the task, turn them into an 'instant consultant'. This will ensure that your early finishers will be consolidating their own understanding of what they have just learnt by teaching it to another person. You can let these instant consultants tour the class offering help or get them to sit at the Enable Table so that baffled learners know who to ask for help.

Strategy: Star Strips

Reducing dependency on the teacher is a tough nut to crack in the classroom. Using the teacher as the first port of call when the going gets tough is a learned habit that is especially tricky to break. It's a behaviour which is often the product of many years of training and, most likely, many years of positive results for the learner. They ask, you tell. Even the very youngest learners we teach will be accustomed to going straight to the parental figure in the room to help them when they're stuck. And now that they're in formal education, this parental figure is you.

Star Strips is another strategy to raise learners' self-awareness about what they do when they're stuck, and to help them stop and assess the worth of the question they're about to ask. If throwing their hands in the air and waiting for someone to save them – like some broken-down car waiting for the AA – is the key strategy they have so far used to help themselves through their time in formal education (and perhaps in their personal lives, too), it is obviously a habit that we need to break. So, how can we get them to stop and think, 'Is asking Mrs Squirrel the only thing that can help me right now, or could I access a different resource?'

The prep is simple: each learner gets a strip of paper with a predetermined number of stars (or any other shapes you choose) on it. Front-load this activity with explicit discussion about changing the class's habits in relation to the kind of questions they go to the teacher or teaching assistant with. The purpose is not to eradicate requests for assistance, but rather to get learners to consider at what juncture the assistance is *necessary*, and not just desirable. It is important to let them know that help from the adults in the room is readily available, but that they also need to consider other resources in the classroom that could help them too. Possible resources in the classroom that they could be encouraged to access are of the same ilk as 3B4Me: displays, textbooks or reference books, purpose-made resources that you have provided them with in the lesson, their own notes and prior work in their exercise books, re-reading their own work carefully, the Enable Table (see above) or asking a peer. If learners have carefully considered all the other options at their disposal, they can then ask the teacher or support assistant for some help.

If the learner does resort to (or require) teacher assistance, the teacher then cuts off one of the stars from their strip. If you feel that snipping off the star is too final a process, learners can simply fold it under or you could put your initial by it to indicate that it has been 'spent'. The idea is that if all the stars have been spent, they are out of opportunities to ask the teacher for assistance. Of course, we would never deny a learner who has a genuine need for support just because they had spent all their little paper stars. The purpose is not necessarily to put them on a question budget, but rather to get them to think very explicitly, 'Is this question worth spending a star on or could I try something else first?'

This strategy is perfect for those learners whose question is, more often than not, 'Is this OK?' Their co-dependency is more about getting you to check over their work at frequent intervals throughout its composition rather than asking explicit questions – and from a feedback perspective this is a very detrimental learning behaviour.

> Co-dependent learners rely on validation even to compose their work. While genuine confusion about whether a task is being approached correctly is a perfectly apt situation to ask for a teacher's assistance, simply seeking a comfort-blanket statement like, 'Yes, that's a great start!', is not.

Star Strips can be one way to illustrate to co-dependent learners, in a very concrete way, the level of support they are seeking over the course of a lesson and to think about whether or not it is necessary.

The strategy can work very well in group or paired work situations, where learners can consult each other about the 'worth' of a question and rely upon one another to seek out the solution themselves. The question, 'Can I spend one of our stars?', will lead to a conversation about the question or query, and opens up the possibility of the group working through the problem together.

It's easy to see how using the strategies outlined in this chapter can significantly reduce the unnecessary teacher-talk that can often tie you up and keep you from more important things. However (worries that last little voice of anxiety in your ear), what about the *explanation* part of the lesson – the part which it often turns out some of them weren't listening to? How do I get that important information into their heads? And what about all this stuff in the syllabus that I've got to get through before the end of the year? How will I ever do that?

Never fear – you'll find the answer to all of these questions in the next chapter.

Chapter 8

Getting Through It All

Embedding Understanding Without Over-Using Teacher-Talk

There is a dubious little phrase that we've all uttered (or perhaps shouted) at some point that metaphorically reverberates from the walls of our staffrooms, classrooms and sitting rooms alike: 'I've got so much to get through!'

'How is this dubious?' you may be thinking. 'It's true!' Yes, it may well be true, but let's consider the connotations of the phrase. 'Getting through' a syllabus implies mere survival, toleration and slog. While each of those may be an absolutely valid response to elements of our workload at times, it is concerning if this summarises the bulk of the knowledge, skills or understanding we hope to pass on to our learners over the space of a lesson, term or even an academic year.

This mentality is rife with problems:

■ If it's the slogging sentiment behind *getting through* that asserts the greatest influence on our planning and delivery of a lesson, how can we expect learning to be embraced with the rigour and commitment we need from our students?

■ If we are *getting through* content, how can we expect that it will be embedded and useful in future contexts?

■ To what end point are we *getting to*? Is it surpassing the hurdle of a specific skill or unit, or is it a greater problem of the sheer volume of content that we feel we're battling against? If the hurdle that we're pushing towards is simply the content we must cover before the end of the year, *getting through* that sounds like an epic and stressful haul that requires a paradigm shift.

There is no denying that there is pressure to cover a lot of content at all key stages and in all disciplines; and with the added pressure of examination results and syllabuses, the stress is further exacerbated. It is when the spirit of getting through it all translates into a top-down dissemination of information that it becomes worrying. This does not necessarily imply that the teacher stands at the front of the room and lectures for 60 minutes, but it might mean taking too much ownership of the learning or guiding with too heavy a hand.

Although scaffolding learning is important for learners to be able to access it effectively, especially when a concept is new and unfamiliar, scaffolding that is too rigid or prescriptive will not leave space for learners to *think* about the learning they're undertaking, and instead they may just go through the more superficial (and forgettable) process of *encountering* the information. This is not to reduce the value of teacher expertise in providing information and instructing on skills. No one would argue that the teacher is not the most valuable resource in the classroom, but it is dangerous when the teacher becomes the sole default resource simply because they have access to the information that needs imparting and that it is quickly shared when they are the conduit.

Proponents of the 'I've got so much to get through' mindset will heartily insist that there isn't time for 'engaging' activities (where engagement is equated with simply *playing* or *having fun* (the horror!) in the classroom). Engaging learners does not have to mean that new learning is set aside while they find a frivolous way to express what they know.

> **Ensuring that learners are engaged in their learning simply means that they are involved, interested and participating in it, rather than just letting learning happen *to* them. If you have engaged your learners, then you have captured their attention – and progress will therefore happen more quickly and easily.**

The paradigm shift to embrace when you feel overwhelmed by the feeling that you just need to get through it is that seeking engagement for your learners is not a bolt-on extra you do when you have time. We don't 'reward' our learners with something engaging to do when we've completed a unit or topic in a timely fashion and can afford it. Instead, consider how you can cover the skills and content in a way that ensures that your learners are part of the process (and we don't mean simply sitting in the same room!).

So, how can you get across the information that you are required to without acting as the mouthpiece for it?

The Hook

Even for teachers who are not generally prone to talking too much, there is still one part of the lesson that's a sure-fire moment to set our eager tongues itching: *the beginning*. Perhaps this is because instruction-giving and explanation seem to lend themselves most naturally to talk.

The problem with this is that while our instincts are telling us to talk a lot during the exposition of our lessons, we are, in fact, very quickly losing the attention of many of our learners at a stage in the lesson when it is most crucial that we capture their interest and secure their investment in the learning opportunities that will follow.

Many perfectly reasonable human beings make up their minds about whether they are going to like and commit to something new in the first few minutes. We do it when we meet new people, when we watch a new TV series, when we flick through a book in a bookshop. Our learners are the same. Yet, too often, teachers feel bound by protocol and tradition to make these first significant moments the most boring of the whole lesson. Instructions like, 'Copy down the learning objective', can often prevail at a time when we should actually be 'hooking' in the learners with intrigue, awe and wonder – convincing them that this is going to be a lesson worth investing some effort and thought into.

You may be wondering, 'But how are they going to know what to do if I don't spend 10 minutes explaining it all to them?' So, how can we avoid an auditory learning marathon *and* be sure that our pupils will not be lost and confused? We have devoted a whole section here to strategies that can be used at the beginning of a lesson to introduce a topic, share learning objectives and capture the hearts and minds of our audience – without defaulting to factory-mode teacher-talk.

Strategy: Teachers on Film

Have you ever found yourself giving instructions over and over again – for the benefit of those who require clarification, who arrived late or who just simply weren't listening? On top of this, some instructions just seem to require repetition in order to get them embedded in learners' minds. Imagine somebody showing you, or worse, telling you, just once, how to knit and then expecting you to be able to produce a bat-wing, roll-neck jumper with Rudolf's face on the front!

When you know that a particular skill or concept is going to need repeated reinforcement, try making a short video clip of yourself clarifying the process through demonstration or careful explanation. Once you have introduced the task live, and your learners are embarking on the activity, set the film playing on a loop. If you think that having a video clip playing in the background is going to be intrusive, then let us assure you that it won't be for your learners, who are children of a generation where background audio and visuals are as commonplace and unremarkable as drizzle on a British seaside holiday is for us.

With the short demonstration/explanation playing on a loop, not only is the information being unavoidably reinforced, but learners are also able to access it, or not, as and when required. The teacher, during this time, is rendered as free as a bird. You can circulate, intervening to support where you deem necessary, and stretching the most able where relevant.

We first saw this technique used in a maths lesson where the teacher had made a short film of himself folding a piece of paper into a series of two-dimensional shapes while providing an audible running commentary on the properties of each formation. The clip was filmed very simply, using the video camera on a mobile phone. The learners' task was to emulate the folding and follow the instructions in the commentary. Since the film was playing on a loop, they were able to do this at a pace most suitable to them. In other words, learners could slow down when they found something tricky and, once they had mastered it, they could pick up the task at whatever point the film had reached in the meantime.

Whether your mini-film demonstrates a relevant skill or explains a complex concept, this technique can produce quite extraordinary levels of engagement. What you will see is a class full of learners working at different stages and at different speeds. Some will be pausing to watch or listen to part of the film for clarification, some will be acting on the instructions, but all will be completely deprived of any excuse to say, 'I don't get what I have to do …'

This can be an even more useful resource if learners have access to a laptop or tablet. The clip can then be paused, sections can be repeated or skipped, and learners can really work at a pace that suits them best.

Strategy: Teach Me, Tell Me (and Then Tell Me More!)

There are topics and units in all subjects that require a baseline of rote knowledge in order to be able to engage with the skills and information it demands. In these cases, where key terms or basic skills are required, we can often default to a didactic, teacher-led approach at the beginning of the topic because it feels like the most efficient way to get the information across. However, especially where the point of the exercise is as basic as *knowing* something, such that the information is embedded, the potential for allowing learners to lead is enormous.

This strategy involves learners questioning each other, teaching each other and challenging each other in an activity that engages the whole class simultaneously. Each learner in the class is provided with a card that contains a knowledge-level question and its corresponding definition or answer, followed by an application-level question linked to the initial knowledge-level question. They use this card to begin teaching their peers.

Ask all members of the class to stand up and let them know that their goal is to exchange cards with as many of their peers as they possibly can in the time that you provide. The interactions with their peers are quite prescriptive: they first ask their classmate if they know the answer to the first question on the card. Their classmate has three legitimate answers: say 'yes' and respond to the question, 'no' and have the answer taught to them or 'maybe' and hazard a guess or a partial answer. It is important to let learners know that all three responses are perfectly acceptable and there is no expectation that they should be able to parrot back the answers immediately.

If their partner is able to answer the knowledge-level question correctly, then the learner must challenge them with the application-level question – but this should not be introduced unless their response to the knowledge-level question was secure. After the first learner's question has been asked and answered (or taught), the second learner repeats the procedure with their own card. Once both learners are confident that their respective partners know the correct answer to the question(s) they have asked, they exchange cards and go off to find a new partner with whom they repeat the process and thereby reinforce what they have just learnt.

The transmission of misinformation is prevented in this strategy by the fact that *all* learners have the correct response at their fingertips – there is no need for guesswork in the assessment of their peers' responses. The activity allows for a large amount of information to be shared with the class in a collaborative, learner-led fashion. The task allows learners to build confidence and verbalise their ideas in a low-threat situation. While it might feel very intimidating for a learner to chance an incorrect response to a question in front of 28 of their peers, it is much less so with just one as their audience.

Confidence grows as well over the course of the task as learners pick up information from each other. In the first couple of minutes, learners are doing more 'teaching' of facts, but as they begin to re-encounter the same cards, you will see more learners answering correctly and moving on to the higher-order challenge questions as well. Feel free to grab a question for yourself and join in the activity – it is great for learners to see their teacher involved in a task on the same level as them, plus it allows you to stretch, support and check their behaviour as well.

A unique question for each learner in the class isn't necessary; on the contrary, it can be highly beneficial to have duplicates in circulation as it increases the likelihood that learners will come across the same card a number of times. While they may need to be taught the response the first time, subsequent repetitions will allow learners to respond with partially, and then fully, correct responses.

This does not need to be an activity that requires fiddly resourcing. After some modelling of what you would like the questions to look like and what a knowledge-level versus application-level question entails, a perfect homework task to set learners is for each of them to draw two key terms from a hat on their way out of the classroom and create the cards themselves. When you collect these in the next lesson, have a quick whiz through to ensure that they're apt and, voila! You have a ready-made resource. The added benefit of this is that each learner will have at least one question in circulation that they will be able to respond to without being 'taught' – an empowering feeling!

Try This ...

Here are some ideal ways to make use of this versatile strategy:

- Key terms and their definition, with the challenge of using the term in context.

- 'What is ...?' questions, with the challenge of 'Why is ...?' questions.

- Practising spellings and using the word in context (it is helpful to arm learners with a mini-whiteboard or scrap paper in case they find it difficult to spell orally without a physical cue).

- Translating an English phrase into a foreign language or vice versa.

- A card with a number on one side and a corresponding number of objects to count on the other.

- A letter or phonic sound to recognise on one side and images that represent words that start with that sound on the other.

- Key historical, religious or literary figures, theorists, inventors and a famous quotation associated with them – the challenge is to explore the significance of the quotation.

- PSHE dilemmas and the desired outcome or response (e.g. e-safety, bullying, sexual health, alcohol, drugs).

An alternative challenge along the same lines is to issue all learners with an image. Instead of asking a predetermined question, learners create a question to which the answer is contained in the image. Consider the image below of a Victorian classroom:

Questions that learners might ask include:

- What equipment might be found in a Victorian classroom?

- What did the teacher write on?

- What did Victorian learners write with?

- What were desks made of?

This variation of the activity results in a very different type of challenge, but the ethos remains the same. Initial training in how to 'read' an image is desirable in order for learners to get the most out of this activity, although the skill of both gathering facts from an image and devising questions will also be refined through the process. The other benefit of this alternative version is that access for pre-readers or struggling readers is improved.

Once the activity is complete, and an impressive amount of new knowledge and under-standing has been spread across the classroom, you can really flag up progress by displaying or reading out the same questions that learners have been swapping with each other and asking them to write down the answer to each one.

Strategy: 3/4/5/6 Pictures, 1 Word

We're sure you'll be aware of the hugely popular smartphone app, 4 Pictures, 1 Word, which displays four pictures and asks you to discover the word that links them. If you aren't, your learners certainly will be! This is really easily adapted to the classroom and can be a memorable way to reinforce key ideas. It is also an effective way to get learners engaging with important concepts and generating their own ideas or questions about the topic – so that you don't have to start the lesson by administering lengthy explanations into their little ears.

Let's imagine that the purpose of your lesson is to help your learners to explore Marxism, or light refraction or Ancient Rome. A quick search of your key word or phrase in Google Images will produce a whole host of royalty-free images for you to collate into a collage of visual representations of your topic. Often these images will depict very different things but all of them will be illustrative, directly or symbolically, of your main theme.

By asking learners to consider the collection of images, and use them to guess the content of today's lesson, you achieve a number of important things. First, this activity acts as an effective hook at the beginning of a lesson to capture learners' interest and immediately engage them. Second, by presenting them with some carefully chosen images relating to your key concept you are encouraging learners to consider the topic from a variety of angles. Third, you are able to embed specific points into your learners' memories through the use of thought-provoking visuals. Finally, you are providing an excellent opportunity for learners to debate ideas and collaboratively solve a problem through talk, listening and lateral thinking.

Try This ...

At the end of the lesson, display the images again. Can the class apply their new learning and come up with additional ideas about how the topic they have just covered relates to each of the images?

Strategy: The Musical Clue

This technique really couldn't be simpler, but it can have a dramatic impact on the general mood of learners and the level of intrigue generated. All you need to do is identify a song whose lyrics are relevant to the key learning points of the lesson and then have the piece playing as the learners enter the classroom. Your learners are required to listen carefully and consider in what ways the song might link to today's topic. You might even ask them to guess what the lesson's topic will be, based on the track.

Generating interest among your learners and throwing them straight in at the active-learning deep end are not the only things this task accomplishes. It also encourages some great interpersonal and oral literacy skills: exploring and developing ideas with others, collaborative problem-solving, speculating and reflecting, and articulating a viewpoint. Try playing the music again the following week and ask them what they remember learning in that original lesson. You'll be surprised by the unusually high number of learners who, for once, can immediately tell you. Music can have a profound effect on our powers of recall!

Some subject-specific examples might include:

Subject	Topic	Song	Artist
History	Second World War	'Springtime for Hitler'	*The Producers* soundtrack
History	Second World War	'Nautical Disaster'	The Tragically Hip
English	Shakespeare	'Romeo & Juliet'	Dire Straits
English	*The Great Gatsby*	'100$ Bill'	Jay-Z
English	Punctuation and grammar	'I Love You Period'	Dan Baird
Science	The periodic table	'The Elements'	Tom Lehrer
PSHE	Teenage pregnancy	'Papa Don't Preach'	Madonna
PSHE	Bullying	'Mean'	Taylor Swift
Geography	Environmental concerns	'Don't Go Near the Water'	The Beach Boys

There are lots of strategies in this book that support a learner-led transmission of new information (getting the important stuff across without bending their ears!). If this is something you're especially interested in, you'll also want to check out: The Walking Chocolate Bar (Chapter 1), Lost Property (Chapter 3) and Jigsaw (Chapter 7).

Making it Memorable

Covering the vast range of content we are accountable for over the course of an academic year is one challenge that teachers must manage. However, once we have covered it, how do we ensure that learners remember it? It is one thing to *present* them with knowledge, but how do we *embed* that knowledge? Providing learners with opportunities to rehearse and reuse knowledge, skills and understanding is key to making it memorable and increasing the likelihood that they will be able to draw on those skills with ease later on. Try some of these strategies as ways to get learners to purposefully revisit their learning.

Strategy: Guess Who?

This strategy is based on the popular children's board game bearing the same name – the premise is the same too. Learners, in pairs, are provided with identical grids of images or key words and asked to choose one square, keeping their selection secret from their partner. (If you think you may have learners for whom honesty is, ahem, a challenge, have them discreetly jot their choice down on a scrap of paper.) Learners then take turns asking each other 'yes' or 'no' questions in an attempt to narrow down the choices in front of them and solve the 'mystery' of which image or key word their partner has chosen. If the grids are laminated, learners can use board markers and cross out images or key words as they are eliminated. If not, a small handful of dried beans or even just small squares of paper can act as tokens to cover up choices. If the correct response is ascertained quickly, that's fine – learners can simply make another selection and work through the process again.

This task provides challenge in a variety of ways: as they attempt to make eliminations, learners are forced to think about properties of the concepts that make them unique from others in the grid, as well as ways that the concepts can be grouped together. This works brilliantly as a consolidation or revision activity, providing a forum for deep thinking and also a means to identify gaps in knowledge. Make explicit to your learners that the purpose is not solely to guess the 'right' answer but to raise further questions about the topic. It is worthwhile having a debrief with the class that covers the following points:

■ Which images or key words were easiest/most difficult to ascertain? Learners could keep data on how many questions it took them to 'solve' each one.

■ What questions did you ask that proved the most useful? Least useful?

■ Which key words or images do you think you understand best? Which do you need to gain a better understanding of?

Below is an example of a grid that could be used in a GCSE English lesson and examples of how the questioning may emerge. The questions that learners ask require them to have an understanding of the important key words and their properties. In this example, the questioner has been able to make links between the sound, rhythm and popular examples of the poetic devices in question.

Metaphor	Simile	Alliteration
Pathetic fallacy	Assonance	Rhyme
Trochaic foot	Iambic foot	Juxtaposition

- Does your poetic device rely on the way it sounds? (Yes)

- Does your poetic device rely on repetition? (No)

- Does your poetic device rely on specific rhythm/number of syllables? (Yes)

- Does Shakespeare famously make extensive use of your poetic device? (Yes)

- Is your poetic device the iambic foot? (YES! – Insert deafening applause)

In the maths example below, learners are not only given an opportunity to make very careful qualitative observations about the 3D shapes in question, but are also able to practise using the terminology in context.

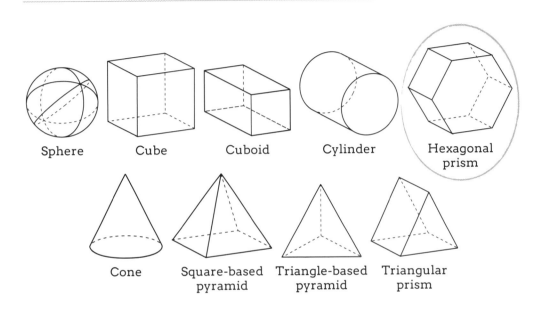

Sphere   Cube   Cuboid   Cylinder   Hexagonal prism

Cone   Square-based pyramid   Triangle-based pyramid   Triangular prism

- Does your shape have more than two faces: (Yes)
- Does your shape have any triangular faces? (No)
- Does your shape have more than eight verticals? (Yes)
- Is your shape a hexagonal prism? (YES!)

Save yourself some preparation work and have learners create the grids as a homework task, identifying for themselves which ideas are most significant or relevant to the topic you have been studying. This in itself is an important learning activity and will consolidate their knowledge. Exchanging grids with another pairing, or comparing with others what ideas they chose to include in their grids, is an excellent way to facilitate discussion about salient points and allow the learners to lead the learning.

Strategy: Tangible Note-Taking

There are no two ways about it: teaching learners to take effective notes, regardless of key stage, is a very difficult undertaking. All too often when we ask learners to take notes on a section of text, what is created is a verbatim copy arranged into bullet points rather than a distilled version of the text. The critical skill of being able to identify key points and represent them in an abbreviated form is easily underestimated. Despite the often poor outcomes, taking notes is an important skill for learners to acquire. The process of note-taking is not only useful for reference purposes, but it is also one that many learners find useful as a means to embed knowledge.

This strategy involves creating a physical set of notes out of Plasticine or modelling clay as an alternative to a paper copy. While this may sound like frivolity and games, what the activity actually does is scaffold for learners the process of distilling a text to its most important elements. By removing the ability to simply copy down the ideas from the text (perhaps in a passive fashion, rather than actually thinking about their meaning), you ensure that learners pay close attention to the key points in the text and think of a physical way to represent them. This does not mean that you ask learners to create a scale model or life-like representation of what they have read, but rather that they create a symbol or simple structure that will remind them of that idea. This is the exact skill that we are hoping to foster when asking them to 'put it in their own words' – they need to devise a way to express an idea in a different form than they originally encountered it.

Consider this example of a text that you might ask learners to take notes on:

Thirteen young men stored 36 barrels of gunpowder in a cellar, just under the House of Lords, ready to blow it up and kill King James I. But some of the plotters started having second thoughts. One of the group sent a warning letter which reached the king. Guy Fawkes was caught in the cellar of Westminster Palace with the 36 barrels of gunpowder when the authorities stormed it in the early hours of 5 November 1605. He was hung, drawn and quartered.

This is a possible output of the Tangible Note-Taking activity:

As you can see, the diagram contains a representation of all the key facts in the paragraph and is represented conceptually – the symbols chosen by the group may be literal, figurative or contain brief letters or numbers to illustrate a point.

> **Tangible Note-Taking has moved beyond an activity where there is potential for simply *copying*, into one where learners have had to think and collaborate on *distilling* information.**

The creation of the 'notes' is best done under timed conditions to prevent learners from becoming too detail-oriented. The purpose of the task is not to make it look pretty, but rather to create a set of cues that will remind them of the important ideas in the text they have just read. The activity is most effective when completed in a group of two or three, as this allows learners to consult each other on what they consider are the most important facts and quickens the pace as the labour involved in creating the symbol is divided.

Once the time is up, ask for a volunteer group to 'retell' the story from their set of notes and have the rest of the class listen out for details they may have missed and/or reported back incorrectly. To keep a record of the notes, take a digital picture and either email a copy to a member of each group and ask learners to print it out before the next lesson or print it out for them. A fantastic test of their memories is to ask them to annotate the image the next lesson. What can they recall from the 'notes' that they took?

While a similar output can be achieved by asking learners to storyboard or draw images of the key points, the impact is not so great. As soon as learners have a pen or pencil in their hand, the temptation is usually to write words. While honing the skill of distilling a text, the modelling clay seems to offer a great advantage in that learners are forced to place ideas in a different medium than the original. For many learners, the slowed-down process of rendering the fact or idea tangible will be the light-bulb moment that makes it memorable.

Strategy: 30-Second Lucky Dip

This speaking and listening technique is just the thing for demonstrating consolidation and understanding of a topic without having to mark 30 tedious paragraphs in your learners' exercise books. It is another limited-preparation gem – you can even use the same bank of key words you've created for What Am I? (see below).

Key words related to your topic are written on slips of paper and placed into a receptacle of your choosing. A learner is then selected to choose a specified number of words at random (three is usually a good number) from the container and then must speak for 30 seconds (or 60 or 90 seconds – whatever you deem suitable for the age or ability of your group) about how those three words fit together, contrast or relate to the topic you have been studying.

Alternatively, you may wish to use this as an opportunity to encourage learners to express strong opinions. Ask volunteers to speak for 30 seconds about why these are the most important key words in the unit, regardless of whether they agree with them. The spontaneity of this task moves learners away from rote learning or simply regurgitating definitions and requires them to think about meaning and how the key terms fit into the unit as a whole.

Providing a small amount of thinking time may be useful for the learner you have put on the spot to ensure that you receive a well-considered response that demonstrates the best of their understanding. You can easily turn this into a whole-class task by pairing learners and assigning speaking turns to each person in the pairing. You could have the pairings all discuss the same grouping of key words 'dipped' by you, or you could have the main terms displayed on a grid and have pairings roll dice to establish the coordinates of the words they must discuss. You could up the challenge by establishing taboo words that learners may not use in their discussion. Likewise, you could make the task more accessible for some learners by providing sentence stems to aid in the structure of their talk.

Strategy: What Am I?

This strategy is an adaptation of something you have probably played as a drinking game while at university or, perhaps more wholesomely, at family dinner parties. The premise is simple: each learner is given a key word, symbol, image or short phrase written on a sticky note. These can be pre-prepared by you or can be created by members of the class on the spot. Without looking at what it says, learners attach the sticky note to their forehead and must then seek out explanations or hints from their classmates that will help them to ascertain what the note on their forehead says.

There is no truer sign that a learner understands something than being able to clearly explain it to someone else – and this is exactly the ability that is being applied here. Learners are engaged two-fold: not only are they gathering hints and clues to work out what their sticky note says, but they are also providing hints and clues to their peers. This discussion from both angles will embed the knowledge and concepts for the learners as they clarify and articulate their understanding around the ideas. And it need not be a one-on-one interaction. This strategy works brilliantly with all learners up out of their seats and moving freely between partners or small groups while engaging in numerous conversations about the key terms and concepts on the sticky notes.

It is important to let the class know that the onus is not so much on the person trying to guess their own word, but rather on the people doing the explaining. It is not the fault of the person who still has a sticky note on their forehead that they have not been able to work out what it says – it is the fault of their peers for not giving them clear enough information. As the number of learners with their word/phrase still to be guessed dwindles, learners converge (in a positive sense!) on their remaining classmates to help them guess their word.

The debrief of this task is important. Were there any terms or images that no one could explain effectively? Which clues did learners find to be the most helpful in guessing their word? Which were unhelpful? Did anyone give them incorrect information? Were they given any clues that only made sense afterwards? Why? Asking them to recall the process behind their guessing allows learners to explicitly make connections between the pieces of information provided to them by their peers and their own understanding.

You may wish to try an adaptation of this strategy that shifts the participation from all learners discussing numerous key words or phrases simultaneously, to focusing instead on one word or phrase at a time with the whole class. Choose one learner to put in the 'hot seat' at the front of the class with their back to the board. Out of this learner's line of vision, write the key term or phrase on the board and ask the class to work together to provide hints and clues to the one learner. This can work really well if you put yourself in the hot seat and allow the learners to select a key term, as you then have the ability to tease out explanations, waiting until you have heard all the pertinent clues you want before making your guess.

Strategy: Cross-Curricular Found Poetry

Yes, it's true: poetry is not just for the English classroom any more. Before you objective-minded people roll your eyes and move on to another strategy, at least hear us out. 'Found poetry' is simply the composition of a poem using exclusively words that you have 'found' in a specific location. This could be anything from a packet of cereal to an instruction manual. Challenge learners in your class to compose a topic-based poem using only words from a source that you provide them with. The source could be a page from a text-book, an entry on a relevant website or a magazine or journal entry – the choice is yours. This includes not only the subject-specific words that they will likely be drawn to, but all the filler words as well. (Remind them that poems do not need to rhyme and can take on any form that they wish.)

Learners will be forced to distil the information from the text you have provided, expressing it in a creative way. This also allows you to step back from a didactic discussion of your text. It is useful to ask learners to justify the word choices they have chosen for their poems and also to consider the words they have not included. Your learners' choices will lead the class discussion through a great alternative to bland end-of-chapter questions. Encourage them to use poetic techniques they may have picked up from English lessons to make some great cross-curricular links.

Here is an example from a science lesson examining the digestive system. The source text provides information on the function of the pancreas.

The pancreas is a gland organ located near the liver in the abdomen. As part of the digestive system, it produces important enzymes and hormones that help break down foods. The pancreas has both an endocrine and an exocrine function, releasing juices directly into the bloodstream and into ducts.

Digestive juices, also called enzymes, produced by the pancreas are secreted into the small intestine to aid in the further breakdown of food after it has left the stomach. The pancreas is also responsible for producing the hormone insulin, secreting it into the bloodstream to regulate the body's glucose (sugar) levels.

And here is the poem:

Pancreas (a haiku)

Enzymes, hormones break

down food in small intestine.

Bloodstream, ducts, insulin.

A haiku is a Japanese poem, usually about nature, that must follow a rigid rhythm of five syllables in the first line, seven syllables in the second line and five syllables in the final line. This is an interesting genre to choose as words must be selected very carefully in order to not exceed the constraints of the form. This example has forced the learner to examine the text carefully and choose the words and principles that carry the most meaning. Justification of their word choices and how the words chosen cover all the salient points is a must. This allows learners to articulate their thought process, further embedding their understanding and making the learning memorable.

Here is another example:

Pancreas (an acrostic)

Produces enzymes and hormones to further break down food

Abdomen, located in

Near the liver

Called to regulate sugar levels by producing insulin

Responsible for breaking down food after leaving the stomach using enzymes

Endocrine and exocrine function: secretes to the bloodstream and the ducts

As part of the digestive system, it is important

Small intestine, digestive juices are secreted into.

Not a particularly subtle or artful form of poetry, the acrostic is a type of poem where the first letter of the first word of each line vertically spells out a word. This is a good form to suggest for learners who need tight constraints or guidance on structuring a piece of writing. Again, in order for learners to create their poem, they must very closely scrutinise the source text to select their words and extract the key ideas.

Of course, there is always the potential to allow learners to choose their own form of poetry to create their found poem, which is an excellent way for them to be creative and engage closely with a text.

Strategy: A Big Song and Dance About It

Have you ever noticed how you can struggle to remember your neighbour's name or what you had for lunch yesterday, but when a song you haven't heard for 15 years suddenly pops up on the radio, you realise that you remember every single word? There is something powerfully memorable about words that are combined with music. We often marvel at how actors can remember all those lines off by heart – and yet just look at the number of lines you can recite if you reel off your five all-time favourite songs in one go! It's a bit like struggling to help obtuse Danielle to remember which side of the line to stand on in PE, only to observe later that afternoon at the school disco that she can perform the entire choreographed dance routine to Katy Perry's latest single, move by move.

With this fascinating phenomenon in mind, a novel and effective way to help learners embed understanding of key information is to ask them to devise a song or dance about the topic to help them remember the crucial elements. (How many of you still have to recite a little ditty in your head to recall the colours in the rainbow or the number of days in each month?! There's also that little number about Hitler's nether regions that has allowed many a GCSE pupil to recall some of the key historical figures in Nazi Germany. For those of you unfamiliar with this one, it is to the tune of the 'Colonel Bogey March' and starts with: 'Hitler, he only had one …')

A structured way to do this is, first of all, to ask groups or pairs of learners to make a list of the key information they will need to remember about the topic – this will form the basis for the content of the song. If there is a particularly important or complex idea that really needs reinforcing, this should be reserved for the chorus and made subject to some repetition! Next, learners will need to pick a song which they feel is especially catchy. This will be the 'ghost tune' to which they will write new lyrics. When they have chosen their ghost tune, they should use their original list to write new words which follow the rhythmic pattern of their chosen song. If learners are brave enough, then have them perform their musical masterpieces for their classmates. Dance moves can, of course, further serve to make the information unforgettable!

You'll soon find that learners are entering your classroom complaining that they can't get the songs out of their heads. For this reason, this strategy is just as useful for sixth-form exam revision as it is for remembering the alphabet in the Early Years!

Try This ...

Let learners record their songs or even produce a music video to go with the lyrics. The video can have the lyrics scrolling along the bottom of the screen, karaoke style, and the learners' choice of images can further serve to make memorable the important information.

Love Teaching

Covering content and embedding understanding for learners shouldn't be about a trawl through work. With the best will in the world, it can certainly feel this way at times but at these junctures, when we feel overwhelmed by what there is to get through, take a step back and think about what really matters. Are you covering it because you have to, or are you providing opportunities for authentic learning to take place? Galloping through a topic without providing sufficient opportunity for learners to get on and do something with their learning will more than likely result in the need for repetition.

So, save some time and put your learners at the helm from the outset!

Chapter 9

Life Beyond the Test

Talk-Less Teaching for Instilling a Love of Learning

Teacher-talk matters. If there is any message that needs to come through loud and clear from this book, it is that teachers are the most important resource our learners have and that the dialogue we have with them matters. The information that we share with them matters. Our subject knowledge and knowledge of pedagogy matter, and sharing this with our learners, through talk or otherwise, is vital.

> **Teacher-talk should never be demonised or denigrated as a matter of course because it is invaluable and it *matters*.**

Although we should celebrate and embrace teacher-talk for the essential tool that it is, we must also bear in mind that not all teacher-talk is created equally. Some classroom talk is superfluous and can detract from the important messages that we want to deliver. To suggest, in a generalised way, that teachers should talk less is akin to suggesting that humans should eat less – it's true for many of us, but it certainly needs closer scrutiny to be helpful or productive advice. Even when this statement is true, it is clear that there are nevertheless some kinds of food that we *should* continue to eat as we have always done, some that we should *begin* eating to improve our health and well-being, and some that we should *avoid* all together. The same goes for teacher-talk.

When a teacher doesn't use their dialogue with their classes in a measured fashion, their words lose power and impact. Too much talking *at* the class results in learners switching off – they know that the information will be repeated or may not even be of relevance, so they choose to occupy their head space with something more immediately interesting. On the other hand, when learners know that what you say counts and that they are accountable for listening to what you say, your words carry weight and value and naturally command attention.

For anyone who has read this book because they were told in an observation that they talk too much, or perhaps have identified themselves as a serial chin-wagger, we hope you have seen that it is the quality – and not the quantity – of teacher-talk that matters. There is not a single strategy in this book that suggests that teacher-talk should be forbidden. We should only be reining it in when teacher-talk is getting in the way of learners making progress.

When teacher-talk takes over in the classroom, the kind of learning relationship that emerges is a parasitic one: your learners are simply taking from you because the opportunities for them to actually do something and give back are restricted. If this image of a learning parasite conjures disturbing urban-legend fuelled images of tapeworms or spiders hatching under your skin, then *good!* This classroom outcome should be just as frightening. What we need to create is a mutualistic relationship, where both teacher and learners are giving, and benefiting, from the contributions being made. Simply creating opportunities for learners to 'show what they know' is not enough, as this can often represent fairly superficial gains in skills and knowledge. These opportunities are important, as small changes ultimately lead to more significant ones, but alongside these chances to demonstrate knowledge we also need to create opportunities to think and do.

We hope we have shown you in this book that there are lots of alternatives to teacher-talk which will not only save your poor voice, but will hopefully help to shift the learning parasites in your classroom into more autonomous learners who can see the advantages of a bit of give and take. And it is exactly this that will develop far longer lasting changes in our learners' skills and abilities.

Embrace An Experiment

If reining in your learning sermon is a priority for you, then you probably have habits to shift that go beyond just the volume and nature of your dialogue with your classes and your personal professional development. The habits of your learners may be a much trickier egg to crack, so you need to start planning for it. It is one thing to tell yourself that you are going to curb your teacher-talk and move more of the responsibility and responses to your learners, but it is quite another to expect them to immediately embrace the same mentality. As mentioned in Chapter 3, our learners establish their expectations of their class teachers quickly – the habits and norms that they experience on a day-to-day basis when working with you become entrenched far sooner than you'd like to think. If you suddenly place very different demands on their listening or participation, you should expect that you may initially meet some resistance.

So, let them in on the plan. If, for example, you know that your talk takes over when delivering instructions, let your learners know that you are going to be changing the way they get instructions about how to do their work. If your goal is to stop repeating yourself and explaining a task three times before letting learners get on with it, you will need to warn them that this is going to happen, otherwise they may very well get caught out as they wait for the alternative explanations. If you are choosing to use a new strategy, like Checklist Challenge or Lost Property (see Chapter 3), to help clarify the instructions or success criteria, let them know that this is the case. They will soon grow accustomed to approaching things in a different way, but just as with any skill we hope to get better at, it will require practice, repetition and review.

You will need to experiment. Start small: choose an element of your teaching that you want to develop and select a couple of strategies that will help you on your way. Plan to trial each strategy in four different ways before you make your mind up about it. It is highly likely that the first time you try out a new technique it will go fantastically wrong or not achieve the outcome you had hoped for. This is not just cause to rip that page out of the book and never look back. It is more than likely a symptom of your learners not knowing how to best navigate themselves around a different approach to their learning and you needing to refine the way you present it to them. Remember that your learners may be instinctively afraid of anything new. They may even, consciously or unconsciously, attempt to sabotage an unfamiliar activity in the classroom because they are uncomfortable with the unknown. Go into a new strategy with this understanding. And remember: don't let your learners' fear of something unfamiliar dictate to you how you teach. Stick to your guns. Let the 'new' become the 'norm'. Taking risks in the classroom is good. Being brave enough not to back off because something doesn't go well the first time you try it is even better.

Eventually, the strategies will become part of your routine, the go-to techniques that you can slot into a topic or lesson because you know that it works. The more tools like this we have in our teaching arsenals, the more streamlined the planning process becomes. While it might take a while to get your head around the logistics of a strategy, and how it best suits you and your learners' needs, once you have identified how to best deploy it, it will become second nature.

The Teacher Is *Not* the Font of All Knowledge

We may be the font of *a lot* of knowledge, but one of the key things that your learners will begin to embrace as you experiment with the strategies in this book is that the teacher's voice is not the only voice with value in the classroom. Unless they are trained otherwise, our learners become conditioned to believe that information shared in the classroom does not have value unless it comes through the teacher. They can easily switch off at the sound of their peers' voices and tune back in when their teacher rearticulates an idea, believing that it cannot be wholly correct until their class teacher certifies it as such (see Chapter 5). This selective listening – the waiting for validation by the teacher before considering that an idea is worth engaging with – is one of the key sins we rectify by embracing strategies that shift the balance in the classroom from one dominated by teacher input to a more balanced approach between learner and teacher input.

While not everything our learners say will be correct (or even topically linked, sometimes!), supporting and encouraging genuine contributions is at the heart of the teaching ethos that we vehemently stand by. Creating a culture of *wondering*, and the comfort and confidence to verbalise it, is a must for drawing learners into the process. A significant part of that is allowing learners to be captured by the 'wondering' of their peers as well. Asking questions, getting things wrong and refining and developing ideas that are 'not quite there' are all parts of the very best learning. Enabling our classes to feel empowered to do all of these comes from experience. Experience of collaboration, experience of being accountable for progress and experience of seeking solutions in places beyond their teachers' support all need to be expressly engineered for the learners, as they will not happen reliably by accident. The brightest ideas do not always come from the most able in the class, so by supporting *all* your learners through the process of contributing to the learning in a lesson, rather than just absorbing it, you can be certain that more of your learners will become a resource, rather than just a passenger, in the classroom.

Think About Yourself

By 'thinking about yourself' we are not calling upon you to become a more self-centred teacher or putting your needs ahead of your learners' ('No homework tonight, kids! I'm off to the pub for my mate's birthday on Thursday and I don't fancy making the time to mark it!'), but rather thinking about your own experience as a learner. This may mean reflecting on your own school experience or perhaps the learning you have undertaken as an adult. What does it feel like to listen for extended periods of time, especially when the topic is not one that inherently interests you, and/or the situation is one you would prefer not to be in?

> **Trust your instincts. If it feels like you have been talking for too long in the classroom, you probably have been. Don't carry on just because you want to 'get through it'.**

There is comfort to be had in lecturing our students because, on some level, we feel that if we have said it, our learners can be accountable for it. There is also a comfort in the behaviour management of talking a lot in the classroom: if you are talking, then the class should be listening. Any student who deviates from this can be dealt with accordingly. No one will debate, however, the fact that, just because you've said something, it doesn't mean that some people have not a) listened to it, b) understood it, and c) bothered to remember it. So take the time to check. Create situations where there is nowhere to hide if they choose option a, b or c.

Think about engagement. As we said in Chapter 8, don't think about engagement as a luxury in the classroom or something that you do to entertain your learners. Think about your own engagement and its inextricable connection to motivation.

> **There is very little that we embrace fully in our lives – when we are given a choice – that does not *engage* us.**

We don't carry on watching if the first 10 minutes of a TV show is rubbish – we simply change the channel. We like to employ the '50-page rule' when reading a book: if it's not engaging by this point, it goes straight into the charity shop box because life's too short and there are too many good books out there. There is a good reason why DIY projects go half-finished in homes around the country: it's because the people who have undertaken them are not engaged by the experience and can't be bothered to finish them in a timely fashion.

> **Ultimately learning is a choice. You can't *make* a person learn something if they really don't want to, and you make it much easier for them to choose to opt out of the learning when they are being taught in a passive way. For learners who do not have an innate interest in studying your subject, or are not intrinsically motivated by education, where is their temptation to take on the learning going to come from?**

We'll say it again: embracing the *engagement* of learners need not be equated with spoon-feeding or dumbing-down education. It is simply about making the learning appealing. Of course, we should approach our subjects and topics with rigour and challenge, but this need never be divorced from engagement. Engaging your learners and creating a learning environment where there is *no choice but to be involved* will ensure that even your most reluctant learners are drawn in.

Think about why you're a teacher (if your immediate thought is about the holidays, then dig a little deeper …). For most of us, we're teachers because, on some level, we love learning. We get a kick out of seeing the changes, micro and macro, in the knowledge, skills and information that our learners gain over the time that we have with them. We take great pride in the achievements of our 'charges' because we know that they are also *our* achievements.

Education, and by proxy, teaching, is not about shuffling through a bunch of content for 14 years so that our young people can wade through some standardised tests and come out with a set of data at the end that might predict what they can do next with their lives. The knowledge that they gain is important, but surely we need to see the journey they take to get to the knowledge as equally important, if not more so. Teaching our learners in a way that allows them to feel challenged, not only by the rigour of the content but also by the ways in which they engage with that content, will ensure that we are not just churning out exam-passing robots, but rather helping to shape young people who will be able to use the knowledge that we've given them in contexts beyond an academic environment. Young people who will leave our classrooms inspired and motivated to know more.

We want our learners to move beyond *tolerating* their learning and, optimistically, we hope that most will learn to love it eventually too.

Sorry, No Cult Status Here

Talk-less teaching is not an educational movement, cult or definitive recipe for success as a teacher. We are not for a moment suggesting that there is *one right way* to be a teacher or to deliver a lesson. We will not be so bold as to offer timed limits on how long we think a teacher should 'be allowed' to talk for or what proportion of the lesson we think a teacher should be talking for, although we have certainly been asked …

Our profession is a blessed one because it affords the flexibility for everyone to do their job a little differently. There are not two of us who could deliver a lesson in an identical fashion because what we do is driven by our idiosyncratic differences as teachers and as people, such that it would be impossible to do so. As a result, a 'recipe' for improving lessons would be inherently obtrusive and perhaps condescending. None of us want to be given pre-scribed, step-by-step, how-to-teach instructions because too many variables would go unconsidered.

Instead, what we have sought to give you are some ingredients, some methods, that will support your individual approach and your unique setting, because *all* of us have unique approaches and unique settings into which common content must fit. Hopefully these ingredients have given you some food for thought.

And now … we'll stop talking.

Strategies

Index

Reach Out 2 Schools
CHARITABLE TRUST

Breaking the Cycle of Poverty
through the Power of Education

Can You Reach Out and Help? ...

Reach Out 2 Schools sends groundbreaking experts into schools in impoverished communities overseas. Our teams work with the teachers and communities to make a real, long-term and sustainable difference to the education the schools provide. In addition to this, we provide the schools with crucial resources to help them make changes that will stand the test of time and forge better futures.

If you or your school would like to support us through fundraising, please get in touch.

enquiries@reachout2schools.com

www.reachout2schools.com

OSIRIS
EDUCATIONAL

Osiris Educational is the UK's leading independent provider of professional development for teachers.

Osiris believes that every child should receive a world class education. Helping teachers in their continuous development is the crucial step to achieving this. We work at the forefront of innovation in education providing pioneering, challenging and effective training solutions.

More than 400 presenters work with Osiris Educational to help teachers improve their ways of thinking and their approaches to teaching.

Some of the most renowned trainers from across the world work with Osiris Educational including: Professor John Hattie, Professor Barry Hymer, Bill Rogers, Professor Viviane Robinson, Professor Carol Dweck, Andy Griffith and Mark Burns.

Our 5 crucial paths to CPD training cover everything from Early Years through to Key Stage Five.

Day Courses:
- Leadership and Management
- Teaching and Learning
- Pastoral and Behavioural
- SEN and Gifted and Talented
- Curriculum
- Ofsted

In-School Training:
- Early Years
- Primary
- Secondary

Teacher and Leadership Programmes:
- Outstanding Teaching Intervention
- Visible Learning
- Mindsets

Conferences and Keynotes:
- Leading Speakers
- Key Issues and Policies

Fast Updates:
- Twilights
- Policy Briefings

FOR MORE INFORMATION CALL 0808 160 5 160
OR VISIT OSIRISEDUCATIONAL.CO.UK